What Was I
Thinking?

Also by the Author

As It Should Be

Westlake Village, Calif.:
Uproar Entertainment, 2000,
CD-ROM 3812-2

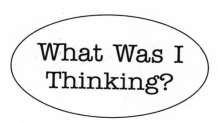

What Was I Thinking?

How Being a Stand Up Did Nothing to Prepare Me to Become a Single Mother

MARGARET SMITH

A Crossroad Book
The Crossroad Publishing Company
New York

The Crossroad Publishing Company
16 Penn Plaza – 481 Eighth Avenue, Suite 1550
New York, NY 10001

Printed in the United States of America

The text of this book is set in 12/17 Triplex.
The display face is Comic Sans.

Library of Congress Cataloging-in-Publication Data

Smith, Margaret.
   What was I thinking? : how being a stand up did nothing to prepare me to become a single mother / Margaret Smith.
     p. cm.
   ISBN 0-8245-2285-0 (alk. paper)
   1. Smith, Margaret. 2. Single mothers – United States – Biography. 3. Women comedians – United States – Biography. 4. Motherhood. I. Title.
HQ759.915.S55 2005
306.874′32′092 – dc22

                        2005019399

1 2 3 4 5 6 7 8 9 10   10 09 08 07 06 05

This book is dedicated to my mother, Barbara Louise,
who continues to dedicate her life to her children.
I hope she never reads it though
because I'll be in so much trouble
I'll have to write another book to explain
why I wrote this book.

Contents

One

Mother Material

*How even when we're done talking about our mothers,
we can't stop talking about our mothers.*

I **THOUGHT,** after ten years of therapy, I was done talking about my mother, but no. It would be impossible for me to talk about becoming a mother without talking about having one. From the moment a girl meets her mother, she begins becoming one, though whether or not she actually takes on the job is up to her. I don't believe having my particular mother made me mother material, not by today's standards. In fairness to her, I have to admit that most of the choices I made as an adult, while holding the reins of my own buggy, also did nothing to prepare me for motherhood.

My mother is generous and kind. She gave me morals and values, a strong work ethic, and the ability to find a bargain anywhere. But the love she taught I've only heard described in self-help books. By today's standards, the love she modeled is obsolete. I know. In my thirties I tried passing it off as love time after time without much success. It would have been easier to unload a shipment of hot combs. My twenties were more fruitful. I only connected with people based on mutual pain. So that kind of relationship was plentiful. No one I knew was interested in mental health. There were many very colorful damaged people to choose from. The universe will dump bargain bins full of them at your doorstep if you so much as raise a hand.

They say there's no greater love than that between a mother and her child. I wanted to become a mother because I wanted to know about that kind of love. My own mother taught me a lot of valuable things, but none of them were love — well, not the kind that anyone would ever recognize as love. She was a shadowy figure in my life. By the time I was seven, I was one of six kids. There was less than a year between my younger sister and myself. Sometimes I wonder if that's why she was on the sickly side as a child. I took the last of the fight from my mother's body, and there was little left for my sister to enter the world with.

When you are one of six kids, part of a brood (I think a brood is four or more kids), a certain amount of neglect is built in. One woman is not enough to go around.

One of my mother's favorite sayings was, "I've only got two hands." The negative aspect of neglect is talked about a lot in books with names like *Your Troubled Teen* and *When Kids Aren't Kidding*. I made them up, so don't go looking for them. You don't have to be one of six kids to be neglected. There are "only's" who are neglected too, I'm sure. Because I was one of a brood, I find overly attentive parents much scarier than neglectful parents. A mother or father hovering over a kid going, "Honey, don't order the pasta primivera. You had that for lunch yesterday and last Tuesday. Why don't you get some nice Bolognese sauce instead of the same thing all the time? It's more interesting. It's not good for your palate to have the same experience all the time."

Nothing makes me more grateful that I was neglected than hearing a kid get that kind of attention. The opposite of neglect is to be noticed. I went unnoticed and it created some problems for me, but what it gave me was a freedom to roam. Don't get me wrong. At first I wasn't allowed to leave the yard, and that eventually became my neighborhood. I was free to roam with ideas and fantasy and perceptions about the world and the people in it. I wasn't told how to think too much of the time, so I could be myself to a large degree.

I thank my mother for that. I am never bored. I find the world and everyone in it truly interesting.

Of the many things my mother didn't notice about me, the one that tops the list was my period. She didn't ask me if I had got my period until after I'd been menstruating for several years. We were putting groceries away. She was inside the refrigerator door. I was handing her the produce; she was loading it into the crisper. We had a rhythm going. I remember I was handing her the last two cantaloupes when she stopped suddenly, looked at them, then at me, then back at them, then at me again and said, "Hey, did you ever get your period?" It was as if all those pairs of melons made her think of other pairs of round things. Her thought process must have gone like this: "Huh, cantaloupe, melons, breasts, ovaries, reproductive system, period. Hey, isn't she turning sixteen in November? I wonder if she ever got her period?"

I assumed my mother knew I was getting my period because she was psychic. I knew very early on that she was psychic. She never came right out and said, "Margaret, Mommy's psychic." That's not how psychic mothers tell their children about their abilities. My sisters and I just always knew. So why then did she never sense that I had begun menstruating? In her defense I'll admit PMS was a hard thing to sense with me because I was born in a bad mood.

I didn't deal well with her question inside the refrigerator door that day. I was mad at her for not noticing, so I answered her with all the bad attitude I could muster, "Tsst, yeah, like three years ago." How could she ask me something like that standing there with the refrigerator door wide open? How could she expose me against the backdrop of cheap lighting and condiments? She always said we weren't made of money, and there I was having the most sensitive moment of my life with the refrigerator door open. I wanted to scream at her, "Now who's running up the electric bill?"

Love is a phenomenon that no one in my family spoke about. I'm sure that's how we ended up in a family together. Somehow we were rounded up by the universe and thrown into a group, and the rule was that no one leave till someone said, "I love you." We used the word "like" instead of love. I was seven or eight years old when I wrote my first love letter. It was to my mother. I wrote that she didn't ever act like she liked me and she wouldn't even be sad if she never saw me again. (Here's a little tip for any would-be writers out there.

14 Mother Material

Don't make your first written piece a suicide note to your mother, then fall asleep while trying to figure out how to do it with a popsicle stick. You just won't get the support you need as an artist.) She woke me up shaking the letter at me and said, "What's wrong with you? I don't ever want to see anything like this in this house again. Now go outside and play." She was right. Fresh air was just what I needed. There's nothing like a good game of dodge ball to snap you out of a depression.

There's a saying about love that goes something like, "Love comes to those who wait." I think it's true because when I was thirty-six years old, a mere eighteen years after leaving home, my mother told me she loved me for the first time. We were talking on the phone and I told her I loved her. She sputtered as words tried to dislodge themselves from the corridor of her throat, "Well, well, I, I, I, I love all my children." Okay, so she loved me as part of a group. I thought, it's a start. I rationalized, it's not like it's a big group like the Mormon Tabernacle Choir. There are six of us kids so it's a small group, more like the Backstreet Boys.

I don't remember the exact day when I realized that my mother would never tell me she loved me. I only know it was a day. It was the same day I realized she couldn't. If she could have done it, she would have done it long ago. And every day she doesn't tell her children she loves them, it gets harder. How awful it must be for her. And here I am; I can do it, but I'm the waiting one, the resentful one. Which is worse? To be my mother who can't say I love you or to be me who can and won't? I think it must be worse to be her.

I hate it when it's me who has to change, especially when I'm right. But I was laboring under this very old idea: she's my mother; she owes it to me, so she should go first. That's how it's supposed to be. Who am I to change the way it's supposed to be? There's a bumper sticker that says, "Let it begin with me." Whoever has that one on their car, thank you. It resonates with me. I hate to admit it but a lot of bumper stickers do. I told my mother I loved her, and then I had to witness her suffering. As she stammered through a response, I realized it was her suffering that I had been trying to avoid all along. I am not a fan of suffering. Whoever says "I love you" first, it turns out, has to endure the other one suffering. Maybe that's why we have armies full of soldiers instead of peacemakers.

My mother is a good woman. I know for a fact she's a good woman. My aunt Anita, the matriarch of our

family, who is known for her good judgment of character, told me so. One day at a huge Thanksgiving dinner,
my mother stood eating over the kitchen garbage can,
a can the size of most people's outside cans. Her theory
was that it gets so cold in Chicago, who wants to be
running in and out with trash bags any more than
they have to? There my mother was, bent over a fifty-
five-gallon galvanized barrel eating a drumstick. We
civilians sat three feet away around the table eating,
when Aunt Anita called to my mother, "Bobbie, come
on and sit down. You've been on your feet all day." My
mother called back, "I got a pie I gotta get out of the
oven." Aunt Anita leaned over to me, mostly with her
mouth (that mouth could turn corners) and whispered,
"Your mother's a good woman; she never sits."

Two

A Mother in Training

*How having a mother is scarier
than becoming a mother.*

I **THOUGHT** getting my mother's approval would kill me. It wasn't a job I thought I would ever want. I had written so many scathing reviews about her as a mother and now I needed her as a reference. I needed her to affirm in some way that I would make a good mother. And by affirm I mean just don't say anything that will hurt my feelings or tear me down. Above all else, don't bring up my past as I have done so often with you.

In many ways it is better to be dead in my family than to be among the living. The dead are spoken highly of in my family. The dead get the approval they need without asking. The dead can do no wrong. Who was I trying to kid, her or me? I always believed I wasn't mother material. Now I was trying to change an old belief based on who I was into a new belief based on who I had become.

The only thing I had ever become before I became a single mother was a stand-up comedian. I am a single stand-up comedian, mother by choice. It's a title that suggests I like making unilateral decisions. The only thing I ever worked hard at was independence. I worked hard at becoming someone who answered to no one. My philosophy was, opinions are noise; suggestions are opinions without conviction. At one point in my life I believed that I didn't have to die or pay taxes. It wasn't a good quality, just a quality.

How could I, an undeserving wanna-be mother, approach my mother with a need of any kind and survive? First of all she doesn't breathe. I've watched her chest. It doesn't move for long periods of time, and then it does. Out of nowhere, about every third day, she inhales. I'm not sure if she's holding it in for those three days or just letting it out so slowly that you don't notice it. My point is, anyone who can live on so little oxygen is spooky even if she's not your mother.

My mother is a quiet person. She doesn't say much because as she puts it, "If you can't say anything nice don't say anything at all." It's not that she's mean, she's not. She just isn't very positive. When I told her I was trying to get pregnant, her usual pregnant pauses went into labor. She quietly gathered her thoughts much like a storm gathers clouds before it rains. And rain it did. "You're not married. You're alone. You work. Who's gonna help you?" I had anticipated her response and was prepared with a one-line defuser. I told her I'd probably hire a nanny. Apparently there's only one thing worse than an unwed mother and that's an unwed mother with a support system in place. According to my mother, I knew nothing of the horrors of getting help, and she was going to protect me from it. "You can't get help, have a stranger raising that baby. That baby won't know who its mother is."

Doubt and negativity are infectious. I listened to my mother with hungry ears. I thought, "What if she's right? What if my baby doesn't know who I am?" Keep in mind there wasn't even a baby yet. All of this fear was based on imagined reality. Luckily I remembered to whom I was speaking. This woman is not just my mother. She is a person who is more dangerous with a little information than she is with no information. But I did listen because she was the only mother I knew, and I didn't know then what I know now. That a baby instinctually goes to its mother. They never mistake the nanny for you, even if you will it. Take it from me, they can spot the one not getting paid a mile away, so surround yourself with all the help you need because it's harder for them to spot you in a crowd. I think that's what Hillary meant when she said, "It takes a village."

My profession did nothing to prepare me for motherhood. If there were an opposite of mother, stand-up comedian would be it. The field of stand-up comedy is for the self-obsessed. That is the only prerequisite. It was perfect for me. Anyone void of self-obsession should not become a comedian; it is not for the humanitarian. Have you ever seen an unknown on Comic Relief?

This is how life as a stand-up comedian is: You sit down and write about yourself, whether it is your family, your friends, or your convenience store. Your agent calls venues to tell them about you and how great you are, how much the crowd loves you. You're interviewed on the radio, in magazines, and in newspapers, and if you have an ounce of decency you'll give that college kid the interview she needs for her school project.

Finally you go on stage to talk about guess who? YOURSELF. The audience applauds you! After your show you let the people meet you, shake your hand, pat your back, and give you hugs, some of which are full-blown, no-holds-barred hugs. You have to love them; they're crazy about you and sometimes just crazy, period. Then some ask, "Can I have your autograph?" Bless them, they haven't had enough of you. You write your name on a piece of paper or the picture of you that they tore from the bathroom wall.

Eventually they go home. It's quiet. You go back to your hotel room, lonely, in need of a little attention, of all things. You call your significant other for a little phone sex, and what's the first thing out of their mouth? "I was just thinking about you; how was your show?" Aahh! Some comedians must have huge phone bills; in an effort to save money they just take one of their star-struck fans back to the hotel for sex. You've got to admire the thrifty.

Being a stand-up comedian is a profession that requires me to spend a lot of time with people who are obsessed with "making it." They were just as frightened by my decision to become a single mother as my family was. They, however, had only two basic questions. You don't want to be not "making it" for more than a couple of minutes at a time in this business. They would crinkle up their faces and ask, "So when did you decide you wanted a kid?" What they meant was, when did I decide to throw it all away? When did I give up? When did I leave the fold? I liken it to being the first one to leave a cult. It puts the question out there, "What does the defector know that I don't?" The second question they asked was, "So, will you bring him with you to gigs?" I'd tell them, "Yeah, he'll just wait out in the car."

Though my profession did little to prepare me for parenting, it had given me all the "me" time I could take. I was saturated with "me." Any more "me" I thought would make me evil. Have you ever noticed how evil characters are drawn? Their extremities turn in toward them. Their noses and fingers curl back toward that which they think of exclusively, themselves. So I said to myself what my parents used to say to me, "I've about had it with you." I had had it with me. It was time to shift my focus outward. But before I did there was one little thing I did that prepared me for motherhood, my ten years of therapy.

Three

One Little Thing, Before I Forget

*How therapy brought me closer
to becoming mother material.*

I THOUGHT when my therapist told me she had
a balloon business on the side it was something
I could overcome. I was so distracted by the uncomfortable feeling I got when she would introduce me
to her other clients on my way out of her office that I
overestimated myself. Granted I had just moved to Los
Angeles, but I didn't see the waiting room of my therapist's office as the place to network, take pictures, or go
in on a time-share. One day at the end of our session,
she invited me to a Christmas tree lighting party at her
house. I had a fear of families, and there she was trying
to make me a part of hers. My plate was full trying to
figure out who I was and who to blame it on, and all she
wanted was for me to make friends.

The truth is I probably could have overlooked her "one big happy family" approach to therapy and stayed with her if it weren't for the balloon business. Her boundaries bothered me, but the balloon business eventually bothered me more. I just didn't want a therapist who sold party favors. It's not that I went to a lot of fairs or car lots or children's parties, but I went to a few. And the thought of running into her at some outdoor event with strings of balloons on her arms was devastating to even imagine. So I went to our last session and told her, "This is going to be our last session." For the first time she looked wide-awake. But too little, too late. I didn't tell her why. I didn't want to let the air out of her enthusiasm about balloons so I simply said, "This isn't working for me." That was over ten years ago.

I found Susan after terminating with that therapist. Susan is a great therapist. She cuts her home address out of the magazines in her office waiting room. She doesn't want her clients to even know her zip code. She doesn't need her clients to be her friends. I think that's a good quality for a therapist to have. I think I have the best therapist in the world, and anyone who doesn't think they have the best therapist in the world is with the wrong therapist.

Ten years of therapy sounds like a lot. It kind of makes finding Jesus sound appealing. I might have gone that route if the nuns hadn't scared me so much. You might say they scared the Jesus out of me. Someone once told me that religion was for people who are afraid of going to hell, and spirituality is for people who have already been there. I think of myself as someone who's already been there. During those ten years I kept busy taking myself apart and putting myself back together again. All of it was necessary, every day of it. I have no doubt that I am better for it. Ten years ago I couldn't have kept a cactus alive, and now here I was talking about having a baby.

Susan asked me why I wanted to be a mother. I immediately clicked into what I call my "higher self" because I thought it had to be a good answer, and my "higher self" is where I go for good answers. I mean, I'm single. What am I doing trying to hang with the big boys, the moms? Who am I to have a baby when I'm still mad that I once was one? Who am I to be a mother at forty? I said, "I want to know what that kind of love is like. I don't want to leave this life without experiencing mother-child love." Then I dropped the breathiness that goes with my higher-self voice (I guess all that oxygen does something to me), dropped back to my good old lower-self voice (much more nasal sounding) and added, "You know, since I never really learned about it with my own mother." I figured if I had been parented right the first time I wouldn't have been paying to sit on Susan's couch. I'd have been sitting on my mother's couch for free.

Even if my mother had been capable of modeling a loving mother-child relationship, I would have experienced it only as the child, not as the mother. Hence I may very well have ended up making the same choice. The difference is that I wouldn't have had such an angry lower self. Don't misunderstand; I adore my lower self. It keeps me busy. It's more spontaneous, makes friends easily, and has a lot of sex.

I also wanted to become a mother because I was almost forty. I saw this time as my last chance. Surely I was nearing the end of my life supply of eggs. I didn't want to be the oldest one at the park. It's the difference between going to the park and going to the park bench. I didn't want to be reading *Mother Goose* in bifocals, and I wanted that car pool lane. Absolutely all of me wanted to have a baby. Not just my higher self and my lower self, but my integrated self as well.

It wasn't just ten years with Susan that helped me become a mother. Certainly, working with a therapist who was a fully formed, integrated person helped immensely. She loved me until I could love myself. She got me closer to being mother material. But my anger about my mother also fueled the purpose. Part of what made me think I could be a mother is similar to what makes a lot of politicians think they can run for office. I've heard senators and governors and even presidents say it. "I thought I could do a better job than the incumbent." I thought, well, I know I'll be a better mother than my mother was; I can't do a worse job than she did. That's what I thought ten years ago.

Since then my feelings for my mother have changed drastically. I still love my mother dearly. But today I am also grateful to have her as a mother. If I had known becoming a mother was going to give me a soft spot for my own mother, I never would have done it. I wasn't looking for a soft spot, never wanted a soft spot. The only soft spot I was interested in was the little one on top of a newborn's head. I never wanted to change my relationship with my mother. I was quite comfortable in a world of blame and judgment, certain that she would notice any day now, explain herself, and try not to cry as she asked for forgiveness. She did try to explain herself once, "Hey, I didn't have the choices you kids have today. If I did none of youse would be here." She never did get to the asking my forgiveness part, and I'm happy to say I no longer require it.

My son brought me a little closer to my mother. It's his fault, but I've stopped blaming him because he's too young to put up a good fight. I'm sure if he were older he would tell me, "Hey, it's not my fault that you two talk every Sunday." And it's not. It's MCI's fault and their five-cents-a-minute Sundays. When all else fails, blame an institution. I'm analytical by nature, but I've learned to leave some things alone because I know if I take them apart and take them to heart I'm going to feel bad. For example, why it is that my mother calls me only when getting a discount? Not even a crisis can dissuade her from her calling plan.

Once my stepfather had a heart attack on a Monday. I didn't hear about it until the following Sunday when I came home to a message on my answering machine. "Hi, it's your mother. Just wanted to tell you your father's out of the hospital. He wants to know why you haven't called him." I guess when you've been psychic as long as my mother has been you forget that others don't possess the gift. She called me once on a week-day. It was alarming. I said, "What's wrong?" She said, "Nothing. Your sister and I are in Vegas. We each get a free five-minute phone call. It's a package deal." Four minutes and thirty-nine seconds later in the middle of a sentence we were cut off. We hadn't gotten to the part about which hotel she was staying at so I couldn't call her back. A few seconds later my phone rings again. I thought it was my mother. Nope. It was my sister, "Hi, I got five minutes. I won ten grand in Laughlin. We took a bus there, it was part of the package...." Suffice it to say I have Sprint. Hey, I said I leave certain things between my mother and me alone; I didn't say I join the parade. Well, maybe I am part of her parade, but I don't ride on the same float. I look at it this way: do I want to be right or do I want a grandmother for my son? My mother continues to grow as a person and as a mother. What more can I ask of her?

Four

Mr. Right

How two wrongs make a right.

I THOUGHT finding Mr. Right would be a breeze since all I really wanted was his sperm. My attitude was, as a woman is it not always a buyers' market? Of course it is. I wasn't involved and could pick anyone I wanted. That would be the easiest part. Then I remembered, wait a minute, guys are sensitive now. What if he wants to actually participate in the parenting? I'll have to get him to sign an agreement. Then I thought, what about HIV? It can't be just anyone. It has to be someone who's not sexually active. That pretty much leaves the comatose. Yeah, I could do a Garp thing. Nah, with my luck the guy would wake up and want to see me again. I have a way with the unavailable. There I was again in my lower self, buying into that whole scarcity philosophy. My higher self, however, knew that the world is abundant. There's plenty of sperm out there.

My search for Mr. Right began close to home. I started looking at my guy friends in a whole new light.

Staring is what they called it. It's amazing how you think your friends are the greatest people in the world until you're window-shopping for sperm. All of a sudden they become a "don't let this happen to you" poster. Without love to blind me in the mating process, I was clearheaded. It was horrible. There was nothing to focus on except their genetic makeup. I became less of a friend and more of a scientist. If I chose someone who possessed what I lacked, I could make the perfect baby.

It was as if I was seeing my friends for the first time. One had a huge forehead, not big but huge. Another had hair everywhere but his eyelids, and another was all torso. The next time you're short on sperm, check out your friends; look long and hard at their mouths. It turns out all my male friends have odd-shaped mouths. They would be talking (I knew because their lips were moving), and I'd zero in on their mouths and think, his bottom lip looks like a top lip. Lips were important because I have thin lips. I couldn't add more thin lips to the brew.

I didn't always stare at them; sometimes I just smelled them. Instead of listening to one friend confide about his devastating breakup, I caught myself trying to place his odor. I noticed that each friend had his very own smell. Did you know people could smell like Campbell's tomato soup?

I soon became an armchair genetic engineer, systematically eliminating everyone I knew from my prospective donor list. If they didn't have a weak chin (another of my genetic shortcomings), they had a poor family health history. Let's face it, if you are the last one alive in your bloodline you are an endangered species, and I didn't want my firstborn carrying the responsibility of pulling a threatened species out of the red. It was hard enough bringing back the spotted owl. It soon became clear. Not one of my friends could right my genetic wrongs.

I had never been a looksist before. In fact I had been accused of the opposite. A boyfriend once asked me why I dated people who were less than attractive. I told him I had never noticed before. After his remark it was all I noticed. I began choosing more physically appealing partners. I don't believe I'm a looksist today. I believe I have preferences, and I don't apologize for them. Men have created magazines full of their preferences and wouldn't think of apologizing. Why should I? Why should anyone?

My sister Sue offered her valuable advice. "Why don't you just go to a bar and pick someone up? None of us [the family] can believe you're going to pay for it." My mother taught us to pinch pennies and look for a bargain anywhere, but you have to draw the line somewhere. Surely she didn't mean sperm. I'm sure she meant everything except sperm. As far as I'm concerned, there's two things you just don't skimp on: your boat caulking and your bloodline. Sue was my mother's prized pupil; she had learned all too well to cut corners, and a bad experience never seemed to ruffle her. She had a unique decision-making style. She meant well, but let's consider the source. I consider a source before I consider a suggestion.

Five

The Source

How shoe polish and a quick horse
do not a cowgirl make.

I THOUGHT older sisters were supposed to be role models. It's a comforting idea, one that attracts me like a clean, soft bed with lots of pillows does. My sister Sue, however, was more like a pool float than a soft bed. A lot of her ideas could only hold air for so long.

When we were kids Suzie got an invitation to go horseback riding with a group of girls that she desperately wanted to have as friends. I think I was about eleven and she was thirteen. She had never been on a horse. The group of girls all had cowboy boots. Suzie did not. She begged my mother to buy her a pair. My mother said, "There's plenty of boots up there in the shoe box. Those black ones are like new." The shoes in our shoe box were all out of style because my mother only bought clothing that couldn't be destroyed. Shoes were no exception. They never wore out. Everything in that shoe box had outlived its owner's love and was now a source of embarrassment.

The boots my mother was referring to were extra special. They were out of style when she purchased them. Out of style, that is, for girls trying to fit in with a cool crowd, not out of style for elderly Hungarian immigrants. They were the only boots remotely resembling Western wear. They were black, fur lined, rubber soled, round-toed boots. My sisters hated them when they got them, never wore them, and grew to hate them even more over the years. They were my favorite boots ever. I couldn't wait for the cold weather to come so I could wear them. They made my heart race. They made me feel powerful, like I had an important job, a purpose . . . and best of all they protected me. They were thick. They could take a nail in the bottom and allow me to walk on unscathed. I was unstoppable in those boots. When my sisters refused to wear them, I was elated. I grew into a new pair every winter, never tiring of them. I wore that same boot style my entire childhood. Suzie felt strongly about them too. "I wouldn't be caught dead in those."

Suzie tackled the shoe box with both hands. She fished around blindly up to her elbows. She pulled one boot up from way down on the bottom and set it next to the box. We stood around watching as she searched for its mate. She was in up to her shoulder now. Her eyes lit up. She recognized something from touch and had ahold of it. Up, up it came from the sea of discarded shoes. It was like one of those scenes you see on the news today when they pull a toddler from a drainage pipe. The only difference was, we didn't clap when we saw the boot come out. We stared, though. How can you not stare at a pair of white go-go boots? I'm not sure how something fashionable and flimsy made it past my mother, but there they were. They had seen their fifteen minutes of fame. They were in style for about six months, about as long as Nancy Sinatra's hit "These Boots Are Made for Walking," then no one on the planet would admit they had ever owned a pair. The poor things had seen fit to fold over sideways above the ankle, flash in the pan that they were, as if the inevitable fall that follows fame was too much for them.

All of us, my oldest sister, Kathy, Suzie, my youngest sister, Debby, and I stood around them. We weren't looking at anything that Dale Evans would wear. At least three of us wondered, "How is she going to pass those off as cowboy boots?" Debby, on the other hand, saw only hope. She was the meekest of my sisters. She loved us without reason. "I like them," was her opinion. Unfortunately her opinion never counted because it came from the heart. It wasn't reality-based. Big decisions were really up to Kathy and me. Kathy had trouble trusting her own experience, so she always looked at everyone else to see what they thought. She said, "I don't know, what do you think?" I said, "I wouldn't wear them." She came back with, "But you wouldn't wear them even when they were popular." Suzie looked to Kathy and said, "Yeah, she only likes those ugly 'guy' boots."

Suzie had two obstacles. One, she had zero budget, and two, most boots didn't fit over her calves, so a budget would not have mattered anyway. That was her main problem with boots. Most of them didn't fit around her calves. Remember, this was back in the early sixties when big girls had no rights, and that meant no boots. She had a decision to make. Either she wore the go-go boots or she declined the invitation.

She painted them with several coats of black Kiwi shoe polish, shined them up real nice, and once again called us in to see them. Once again we stood around

the boots. This time we were in deeper. We were con-
cealing, covering up, and could be found out. Well,
Suzie could anyway. She waited for the verdict. Debby
thought they smelled good. They did. Who doesn't like
the smell of shoe polish on leather? Kathy said, "Well
... they look better ... I think. Don't you think? No one's
gonna look at your feet anyway." We all knew that was
a crock, but I was willing to build on it because it was
all we had. "Stand back there," I told her. She walked to
the other side of the room in them and stood against
the wall. Kathy and I looked again, giving ourselves
a moment to digest the bad news. They looked just
as bad farther away. Then we did something that is
never a good sign during any inspection. We started
backing up.

My sisters and I were always backing up and looking
at one thing or another. Kathy and I started discussing
the reconditioned boots with Suzie waiting at the wall
for our verdict. "I think if she wears long pants...."
"...And stays on the horse." "She could just ride ahead
of everyone." "Yeah." We looked at Suzie and I said,
"You're gonna need a quick horse."

Who knew it would rain the day of the ride? Suzie
rode hard and came home wet. As for the boots ... well,

the mud, the rain, the giddy-upping—five coats of polish just wasn't enough. There was a little polish left on the tops. The bottoms were once again white. The color that made them famous was back, but the go-go was gone.

Six

The Suggestion

How every story tells a picture.

I THOUGHT about my sister's suggestion more than I care to admit. She wasn't thirteen anymore. She was all grown up and had changed since we were kids. She wasn't as desperate for friends as she once was, but her denial system was just as powerful. I call it a denial system. Maybe she just thinks more positive than I do. Metaphorically speaking, I backed up all the way to the wall and told her, "I can't go to a bar and pick someone up. I hate bars. I don't drink. I don't smoke. How am I going to go into a place I don't like without first drinking a lot of vodka, and how do I pick up someone I don't like without a handful of Percodan?" It seemed to me that her fertility plan for me to have a one-night stand was no better than her plan to make those boots work.

Every important decision we make is another story in our lives. The decisions we make regarding our children are not just our own stories but theirs too. I could just picture me one day telling my baby that romantic story when eventually he asked, "Mommy, how did you and my dad meet?" "Well, Sweetie, it was last call up at the Auto Bar. Mommy was ovulating and had on a real pretty red sweater. The bar was closing in an hour so her standards had lowered quite a bit. Your daddy was a sweet talker. I could tell by all the things he was saying to himself. His name was Wayne. Well, I called him Wayne. He looked like a Wayne. He had a powder blue '77 Lincoln. It was in mint condition because with all the DUIs he had, he hardly ever drove it. As luck would have it, he'd been rolled early that night and didn't have any money, so I bought him a drink. Then Mommy helped him to the potty. That's when he fell for me and passed out. He's probably still there, at least his car is, but Mommy had to go home and wash the smoke out of her hair so she could make a beautiful baby like you."

I couldn't do it. I didn't want some "woman meets weirdo" conception story for my baby. Whatever my plan ended up being, it would have to make a good story. I'm no stranger to weirdos. I've always attracted them. One night after a show in New York, one tried to convince me he wasn't a weirdo. "You think I'm crazy, don't you?" I admitted it had crossed my mind. He said,

"I'm not crazy and I have papers to prove it." I gave him my manager's number and told him to fax over the papers.

One morning I was doing a radio show and got a caller who said he liked my comedy. He could only be on for three minutes. It was like a call from my mother. I said, "Is this an MCI special?" He said, no, he was calling from the pay phone in a mental hospital and wanted to know if I could talk to some people for him about getting him out. "They'll listen to you," he said. When I told him that I thought only a family member could sign his release, he got real quiet. I thought he was going to break down, and in a way he did. He proposed. Wouldn't it be nice if the story of my baby's beginning didn't star a weirdo and have a supporting cast of freaks? The stories we hear about ourselves coming into the world are ours for life. They affect how we see ourselves for a long time.

My mother tells this story about when I was a little girl. She thinks it's funny. I think the only thing missing is an appearance by Hitchcock. She was out shopping all morning and stopped at Mimi's (my paternal grandmother's) on the way home. I was asleep in the backseat. "I didn't want to wake you up," she says when she tells the story, "I figured you needed the sleep or you wouldn't be sleeping." She went in to visit with Mimi and left me out in the car. At this point in the story she interjects, "You could do that back then. This was back when you didn't even have to lock your house. Not like today." (Our house was also robbed at one point.) Her visit went on longer than she had planned, and she forgot I was out in the car. My mother always says she has psychic abilities, not a photographic memory.

My Uncle Jim came home and asked if he could borrow the car. He had some urgent business he had to tend to up at the bar where he worked. She told him to go ahead and take the car. He didn't look in the backseat and drove away with me asleep. When he turned the ignition off in front of the bar under the Hamm's Beer sign (the "Land of Sky Blue Waters" beer), I woke up. "Scared him half to death," is how my mother tells the story. "Boy, was he mad. Had to drive you all the way back to Mimi's." She always laughs at that part of the story the most. He came in and yelled at her, "How could you forget one of your own kids was out in the car?"

Through a process of eliminating stories that I didn't want to have to tell my child, I came to the realization that Mr. Right was not going to be someone I knew or would ever meet. Our special story about starting a family would have to be one of love and science. I'd find my Mr. Right at a sperm bank. I did some research and found out these guys were right up my alley. They didn't see the point of knowing me either.

The only drawback was that I would be bringing a child into the world who would never have a physical image of the only guy he would likely ever have as a father. Not being allowed to talk about my real father when I was growing up was enough to make me angry at just about everyone I knew and didn't know. I could only imagine how never knowing what he looked like would feel. Plus I wasn't ready to give up my genetic tinkering. If I could see what the guy looked like I could pick a donor who had complementary physical traits and phase out all the imperfections in the Smith genes, like Smith women having no butts. It looks like we have a couple of saltines back there. And while I'm at it, I'd like more of an arch in the feet. Oh, and some olive skin please. We burn easily. A picture would satisfy my lower self and my baby.

When you grow up without your family intact, pictures are everything. We had two sets of family pictures: the set with our stepfather and the set with my real father. The ones with my real father were packed away in a cedar chest after his death. My mother put the chest upstairs where our bedrooms were, away from her and out of my stepfather's sight. I used to sneak into it, get lost in its smell, and go through the pictorial representation of our previous life. A life that was hastily patched back together with a new father. Inside the chest were pictures of my parents' wedding, our baby pictures, pictures of my father with my mother, us with him, and us with them together. He was handsome and hunky, and best of all he had a butt. I know because his wallet was in the chest and it was still shaped to the contour of his body. You don't have to be a forensic expert to know it was rounded because he had a butt.

Inside the wallet was his license, two dollars in the billfold, and some change. There were no pictures of us in there. Maybe someone took them out and placed them in his pocket before they buried him. It would be nice to have a picture for my child. I don't think it's too much to ask. Maybe I should have my agent negotiate for me. He's good. He would ask for half the donor's wages then settle for a picture. Then I could yell at him, "I want a three-picture deal or I'm walking!"

Seven

Doctor, Donor, Desperado

How Duck Duck Goose goes on forever.

I THOUGHT referring to Dr. Cornelius as my fertility doctor instead of by her proper title, infertility doctor, was a more positive approach to take. I needed a fertility doctor before I picked a donor. So I went to see Dr. Cornelius, who came highly recommended. Her success rate was unequaled by any other, except that doctor who was arrested for inseminating his patients with his own sperm. Talk about coming home from the office exhausted. He's now getting all the rest he needs in jail. And you know those mothers wouldn't have pressed charges had the good doctor looked like Brad Pitt. But it was his lot in life to look like, albeit with thick black hair, Larry Bud Melman. It's guys like him who are endowed with Olympian sperm. Their sperm is genetically coded to succeed. It has evolved to compensate for looks. In other words, it knows it's only getting one chance, so it could bounce off a wall onto a woman's thigh and still army-crawl its way to her vagina if it had to. Brad Pitt on the other hand doesn't even have to have sperm. Dust could puff out, and he'd still do well. He could have a vagina.

Cornelius examined me and said, "Your levels look great. You're very young reproductively." I liked her immediately. She informed me of options for donors. She had specimens available right there in her office. Patients who had become pregnant and didn't need any more left their extra specimens in her care. It made sense that you couldn't return the stuff, what with all the product tampering that goes on today. This sperm had a successful track record. It was appealing, but I didn't like the fact that my child could be in the same school district with his/her biological sibling. They could meet, fall in love, then find out the awful truth. You've watched the Lifetime channel. The California Cryobank in Westwood sounded like the best idea. It wasn't far from my house. I could actually pick up the sperm, bring it to Cornelius's office myself, and save a few dollars. My mother would be so proud of me. She might even start to warm to the idea of my being inseminated if I could tell her I got a deal.

It was the end of my first office visit. Doctor Cornelius
and I were saying good-bye. She was telling me how
picking a donor is a crapshoot and joking about what
her worst unknown donor nightmare would be, sperm
with a Kevin Bacon nose. I said, "Too bad none of these
places offer pictures." She said, "Oh, there is a place
that's doing that now. They just sent me some litera-
ture. I think you pay a little more." Cherubs came from
behind clouds with harps and sang songs. The universe
was providing for me. I was elated. (I don't know why I
say things like "I was elated." It's not like I look elated
or act elated when I'm elated.) Everyone I had talked to
had told me a picture was impossible, that donors must
remain anonymous, that they don't want you to know
their names let alone give you a picture. There were
whisperings of a select few donors who would allow
contact at the child's request when she/he turned eighteen. I was told there might be a contact clause in the
event of a life-or-death medical emergency. Now it was
all a bunch of bull, old information. Such is life in the
fertility business. Cornelius handed me the brochure
that made the cherubs sing and cautioned me, "It's in
Georgia so it's not as convenient as something local."
Yeah, yeah, yeah. I thought, by the time I get home that

could be bull too. I left her office with folders under my arm, the world smiling on me and the universe saying "Cheese."

I called the firm in Augusta, Georgia, and requested their donor list. A few days later it arrived, five pages of Mr. Rights. At the top it read "Fall 1994 Donor Listing," and it had a donor number and nine columns of description: race/ethnic origin, hair color, hair texture, eye color, skin tone, blood type, height/weight, occupation, and interests/religion. An asterisk next to the donor number meant the donor had washed sperm for intrauterine insemination, and a pound sign meant a photo was available. I scanned the list for pound signs. There was one, then another. They all had straight hair. I wanted curly. It read straight hair, straight hair, straight hair, and straight thinning hair. I thought, "What is going on?" Then I saw it, a pound sign with brown curly hair, blue eyes, fair skin, O-positive blood type, six foot one, 190 pounds, occupation/Electric company. Okay, it's not exactly a career, but it is a job and he's probably perfectly happy at the electric company. He could be an engineer, or maybe he touched some bare wires and has a nice desk job now. Then I noticed

the interests/religion column: fishing, hunting, base-
ball, and Church of God. I don't know about you, but
I can't read the words "Church of God" without hearing it in a deep fire-and-brimstone voice: "CHURCH OF
GOD!" My thought was, No way am I putting redneck,
Christian right (or as I call it, Christian Reich) sperm in
my body.

There was my lower self again. It takes very little
trepidation to send me into a downward spiral. I have
downward spirals all the time. This one went like this:
"I can't believe I have to ask someone for sperm, let
alone pay for it. They wanted two hundred bucks a pop.
Was it cheaper in college or what? I was practically
tripping over the stuff. Now look at me, calling out of
state during peak rates for some and begging for a picture. I probably won't even be able to see what he looks
like in the picture. He'll be wearing a white hood. I'm
pathetic."

It's interesting trying to experience a person based
on a few facts written on a piece of paper. That "just
the facts, Ma'am" approach was bringing out the worst
in me. It's the same approach we use in our courts of
law. The defendants have to sit there like a cardboard
cutout — silent so they don't stir our juices and affect

our judgment. What's in a personality anyway? Who is donor 666 without the distraction of a flirtatious comment or a crooked smile to animate his DNA? He is hidden in that reduced state of being recorded on a donor profile sheet. How many dates would it take to find out that the guy you're seeing goes to the Church of God? Not as many as it would take to find out he's in the militia.

"Hi, I'm calling about donor BFM 9059." I told myself BFM stood for big f-----g male. "That comes with a picture doesn't it?" She said, "Well, let's see." I could hear her shuffling papers. Probably the same ones I have in front of me, I thought; I'm one step ahead of her. I said, "I have the list. It says he comes with a picture." I immediately had this fantasy of her saying back to me, "Well, if you put it that way, they all come with a picture don't they? I think this one used *Playboy,* December's centerfold. Yes, I remember because it was around Christmas time." But that's not what she said. What she said was, "We're out of BFM 9059." I had never even considered the possibility of rejection. Here I was all vulnerable, expressing a need, and boom! I hear a big fat "No." It was as though she had told me someone almost-but-not-quite close to me had died. I was filled with disbelief. "There's none left?" I said in my pathetic Kübler-Ross first stage of grieving voice. "Yes it's been discontinued." Who has time to grieve on long distance during peak hours? I hurried into another Kübler-Ross stage, anger. "Let me get this straight. You're not getting any more?" "That is correct." I was now in the final stage of grieving, acceptance. Surrender always puts me in touch with my higher self. Now I wanted to be nice to her. Did we not both suffer? On some level I guess I thought we were in the same boat. I didn't have any sperm, and now I saw she was capable of running out too. Compassion has a way of quieting the mind.

I was much more casual now, as I often am after a devastating loss. I said, "I have a couple of others circled that look interesting." I was on the rebound. The donors had become just "interesting." I would probably never get so attached to another one. "What about BGL 9276?" "No, we're out of that." "How about BGL 9220, thinning hair; you must have a barrel full of that." "I'm afraid we're out of that too." There wasn't a hint of regret in her voice. "If you're out of everything," I asked, "why bother to answer the phone?" Silence.

"Will that be all?" I hated her. You give some people a little power and they can't handle it.

I went to the wastebasket and took out a wadded-up piece of paper. I uncrumpled it and queried, "CFN 8848?" It was reminiscent of last call at the Auto Bar. I figured, what the hell; they're probably out of it anyway. It was a policeman. I picked him for the photo quality. From a kid's point of view, he'd look real important in the uniform. The unborn have never seen the Rodney King video or read about the Rampart corruption scandal. She said, "We may have some at our other location." Not bothering to cover the phone, she yelled to someone, "Bobby, do we have any CFN 8848 over in Emmit?" That was a little unprofessional, I thought. Then I figured, What's one little red flag? She said, "While he's checking, is there anything else you're interested in?" I told her, "Not really." The rest were pictureless or had brown eyes.

I waited. I hadn't realized there wasn't a pair of brown eyes in our entire family until my manager pointed it out to me at my family reunion. "Does your family have something against brown eyes? I'm the only one here with brown eyes." I had begged her to go with me. It was back when I couldn't face my family

Doctor, Donor, Desperado

alone. I paid her handsomely and there she sat at the
picnic table, aware that she had the only pair of brown
eyes there. I forced myself to look at them. We're not
big on eye contact. Not even the extended family in-law
faction had a brown eye amongst them.

I heard a muffled "No" from Bobby on the other end
of the phone. The receptionist relayed Bobby's "No"
because she liked saying no. I wanted to have a blue-
eyed baby but was willing to make one exception. I
had a good feeling about one donor who happened
to have brown eyes. My agent was right about casting
calls. He said, "They don't know what they want." I said,
"What about DFL 8801?" This brown-eyed donor was
pre-med, English/Irish, and possessed a pound sign.
She said, "We don't have any left in the regular, but
there is some in the Blue Line Special."

I flipped through my pages. Had I missed something
in my desperation? I didn't see anything about a special. How would I ever tell my mother that I had missed
the special? "What's the Blue Line Special?" I asked.
She said, "Well, a regular specimen has approximately
fifty thousand spermatozoas. The Blue Line has over
a hundred thousand. It is a bit more expensive, but

you're getting twice the count." I knew from my drinking days that a double costs more than a single, and even if you never drank, any idiot who ever ventured into a Starbucks knows that a double costs more than a single. I needed to hang up at that point. I didn't think I was ready to order the special, and no way was I prepared to say, "Give me the cheap stuff."

Eight

OvuQuick

How thinking inside the box challenged my mind.

I THOUGHT conception would be simple compared to finding Mr. Right. I did not order the Blue Line Special or get the picture I wanted or use the Georgia Sperm Bank. Mr. Right had been right under my nose the whole time. He was at the California Cryo Bank right here in West Los Angeles. He was of Scandinavian descent. A blond-haired, blue-eyed, six-foot-tall Viking. He was right-handed, which means he held the magazine with his left hand and himself with his right. I guess in a way I did get my photograph. It's not a picture I would ever share with my child, but it humanized my donor in a very erotic way. I bought three batches. I was sure I wouldn't need more than that. Remember, I was very young reproductively. I loaded the nitrogen tank with my Viking sperm into the car and tried not to get in an accident on the way home.

All I had to do now was ovulate between gigs and conceive. For one whose timing is impeccable that should be easy. Dr. Cornelius told me to get an ovulation kit called OvuQuick because it was more accurate than the others. It was also more expensive. Fifty dollars. I was upset leaving the drug store. I'm always upset when I buy feminine products. I feel like I've been taken advantage of. Why is it that everything a woman's body does once a month costs her money? Every time I pay four dollars for a box of sanitary napkins I feel taken. I'd rather have someone grab my purse and run. At least then I'd get some exercise.

I think the government should pay for menstrual supplies, including Motrin, or at the very least they should be tax deductible. I've never been associated with any cause, but if I ever am I believe that, if we organize, women could make this happen. I've always admired Dr. King, so it would have to be a peaceful civil disobedience. Women could just bleed in the streets till their demands were met. Every airplane seat and park bench in the country would be marked. It would become the new art form, our very own graffiti. Each stain would represent an angry woman. We would become so empowered we wouldn't need antidepressants anymore. Finally there would be a place outside ourselves to express our anger at a society that charges us for being women.

When I opened the fifty-dollar ovulation kit, the world inside was in black and white. It was a world of science. I saw vials and test pads and cups and droppers, everything but a Bunsen burner and a lab coat. There were directions in there too, which I immediately set aside because directions make me anxious. I would rather rely on 800 telephone numbers. Eight hundred numbers are for people who like to get someone else to do their work. I prefer to save my energy for more important things, like complaining and indignation. I believe in putting things together and then looking at the directions. Even then I only look to see whether they mention anything about having extra parts left over.

My anxiety was at a level reserved solely for nightmares. You know, the nightmares where you can't find the classroom you're supposed to be in and you're late. Then out of nowhere, you realize you don't have a top on, and when you try to cover yourself up with your textbook it turns out to be one of those little horoscope booklets you pick up in a supermarket checkout line. It's not quite big enough to cover you. That dream always ends with me struggling to tear the book in half. That's after I can't get the custodial closet open. I can fear anything if I put my mind to it. I mean, the kit was just a few little things inside a little box. Was I developing a fear of boxes?

My mother had sent me a box a few days earlier. Out of the blue it had appeared on my porch. I looked at it suspiciously each morning when I woke up and again before I went to bed at night. I had no idea what was in the box. It wasn't my birthday, Christmas, or middle-child day, and to make matters worse, the Unabomber was still at large. The box from my mother would have to wait. I couldn't deal with it until I mastered the box in front of me, the box with the ovulation kit in it.

Following directions highlights my shortcomings. All I needed to do was focus, listen, and carry out a simple task. In other words I should pray. I reminded myself that I was a grown woman and would have to read the directions and understand them if I wanted to conceive. Some people light a candle and have a little wine and sex in order to conceive, and some face their fear of directions. Your path is your path, and that's that.

One item the makers of OvuQuick should add to their kit is a package of rubber gloves because only a penis could accurately hit the tiny cup they provide for the urine sample. You couldn't fit a side of coleslaw in the thing, and they expect you to hit it blind. Per Dr. Cornelius's instructions I started testing with OvuQuick on the eleventh day of my cycle. I drew some of my urine up in an eyedropper, squeezed six drops onto the test pad, and began mixing vials of chemicals and timing each one.

A blue dot is supposed to appear on the test pad when you are about to ovulate. I waited for the dot to appear. Nothing appeared. For three days I repeated the procedure. Nothing happened. I decided it should be called OvuSlow. Was I doing something wrong? I reviewed the directions, which no longer scared me. I was in fact ready for more complicated directions. I was so empowered by my ability to run my tiny ovulation laboratory that I could have eaten directions for breakfast. I followed them precisely. I began questioning the manufacturer. Was the kit defective? Should I call the 800 number? I should ask for my money back. Dr. Cornelius told me it could take up to five days before it turned blue. I didn't have five days; I was almost forty for God's sake. On the fourth day, exhausted and hopeless, I got my blue dot. One box down, one to go.

All of a sudden I felt curious about the box my mother had sent. It had sat on my dining room table for ten days. What had she sent that she didn't call to tell me about? I opened the box slowly. I was prepared for anything. I lifted the flaps and saw crumpled-up newspaper. I lifted it off and set it on the table. It maintained its square shape. Underneath was an envelope with a lump of old wax paper inside it. I opened the wax paper and saw two braids of blond hair. It was my hair. My baby hair. Hair that at one time went all the way down to my butt, hair that was about six inches long. I took the braids out and held them. They were soft and had permanent bends in them from lying in an envelope in the fetal position for thirty-five years. I remembered my early blond hair. I hadn't wanted it cut. I remembered that I didn't want my hair cut off and I wanted my dad to come back. I felt sad for the little girl who had worn those braids.

Under the braids were my grade school class pictures. I opened the one that said first grade. I looked so small and scared, like I was ready to fall apart and the only thing holding me in place was fear. I remembered Miss Dobson, my first grade teacher, and thought, "No wonder I'm scared in this picture." She used to chew the ends of her glasses till the enamel was gone and they were gnarled stumps. She would wash our hands way too hard before allowing us to touch the books. She shook kids by their ears if they missed words. Ralph Ward, who missed a lot of words, had the biggest ears in the class. None of the other kids looked scared though. They wanted to be there. I wasn't quite ready to be there. There wasn't enough of me to survive Miss Dobson. It's a feeling I've had my whole life, which I learned at a young age to cover up.

I studied the pictures. I looked afraid in every picture until sixth grade. It only took me until sixth grade to get things under control. I can document it now with that year's class picture. I exuded a "screw you and anyone that looks like you" attitude. In the span of one summer, albeit with a slight hormonal change, I had morphed into a little toughie.

I dug deeper into the box and pulled out several of my report cards. I opened them up one after the other and saw that I was academically only average. Then I noticed that I had checks every year in "fails to listen, fails to carry out simple tasks" and "easily distracted." Were they all byproducts of fear? They were all skills necessary for following directions.

Nine

Conception

*How a good bottle of wine and hot sex works
if you're not me.*

I THOUGHT science would be better than sex. I was on Dr. Cornelius's table at 7:30 the following morning, my head propped up on a pillow. I could see her clearly between my knees. My feet were in the stirrups; I had freshly shaved legs and was sporting my best crew socks. I waited. My sperm was in another room thawing. Ah, life was good. The butcher paper under me crinkled. Add my paper blanket to that and you've not only got patient apparel, you've got a fire waiting to happen. Fire or no fire, I was getting inseminated. They wait until you get there to take the sperm out of the nitrogen tank. Thawing it out after a patient arrives narrows the margin of error. Everything was precise and everyone was careful. They ran their office like Mrs. Stern, my eighth grade home economics teacher, ran her kitchen. The only difference, I hoped, was that here they didn't have to eat their mistakes.

Waiting naked from the waist down with one's feet up in stirrups is not like waiting in line at the bank or the grocery store or anywhere else really. It's much lonelier. I began inspecting my body, starting with the part closest to me, my thighs. I never realized just how white my legs were until I had Dr. Cornelius's tanned face to compare them to. I've seen packaged Cornish game hens at the grocery store with more color than me, and they were covered with feathers their whole lives. I wished I had feathers.

I noticed how blotchy the insides of my thighs were, became uncomfortable, and began the sort of sense-less chatter an accomplice uses to distract witnesses during a criminal act. "I think horseback riding is an excellent way to give a child positive self-esteem," I blurted out. "I mean that they can learn to master something so much larger than themselves." See how anything can happen when I'm feeling fearful? Having nothing to say about horseback riding and its effects on a child's self-esteem, the doctor proceeded to un-wrap sterilized utensils. I interpreted this to mean she didn't like me. I wanted to feel better in this situation, but feeling comfortable with someone between my legs who can't stand me was not a social skill I ever had aspired to achieve even though it wasn't the first time it had happened.

It had happened once before. I was about seven or eight. My mother used to take my sisters and me to the VFW post for our vaccination shots. I don't remember how old I was on this visit. I was at that age where my sister Kathy hated me most of the time. I believe the only time she didn't hate me was when she wasn't home. This particular morning I wouldn't share my banana with her so my day was going to be rocky. I received the usual barrage of name-calling I'd get on a decent day but with more severe faces. "Stingy. Fan teeth. Frizz bomb. Tomboy." Her voice trailed off as we walked into the place. We all became horrified at the suffering that was clearly taking place. There's nothing like the screaming of tortured kids to level the playing field.

We got in a line and waited. Kathy was up ahead because she was the oldest. That banana I had refused to share an hour ago wasn't settling so well. The smell of alcohol, the sound of newborn babies crying, the sight of so many shiny instruments, the feel of my sleeve being rolled up, and the sheer size of the operation began closing in on me. I got closer and closer to the front of the line until I was next. Why was the doctor so happy in the midst of all this suffering? He dabbed my arm with alcohol. The babies sounded far away now. He came at me with the needle. The lights went out. I threw up and fainted. I'm not sure in what order.

I don't remember ever getting my shot. When I came to, I was lying on a table in a back room. The doctor was shouting orders at someone. "Get down at the end of the table and pump your sister's legs. Come on, faster. Get your sister's blood circulating." I looked down between my legs. It was Kathy. There she was despising me and at the same time helping to revive me, giving me the evil eye and pumping my legs as fast as she could. She was the little engine that could hate me.

Dr. Cornelius entered talking, "It should be just about ready." A moment later a nurse walked in with the specimen. She looked at me with a big smile and said, "It's good stuff, a lot of swimmers." I asked, "Do some not swim?" "Oh yeah, they just chase their tails. These are swimming straight ahead," she said as she went out the door. Cornelius drew the Olympic sperm up into a thin tube. She put the tube inside my uterus, and out poured more of my senseless chatter. "How old was your daughter when she started horseback riding?" "My daughter?" she asked with a what-the-hell-are-you-talking-about inflection. Then before I could respond, she withdrew the tube and added, "I don't have any kids!" As though it were the most disgusting thing on the planet. She threw the used tube in the biohazard container. I felt awful that I had insulted her. "Oh, whose daughter is that with the horse in all those pictures on your desk?" She ripped her rubber gloves off. "That's me." She stepped on a pedal I couldn't see, and my pelvis began tilting up. I thought I was being ejected into a bio-bin for the stupid thing I had said about her having a kid that rode horses. The table stopped suddenly. She said, "Lie here for twenty minutes, then you can get dressed," and she was gone.

I heard her enter the next room sounding friendlier than a gay waiter. "Hi, how are you today?" I wanted to think about the baby to be, to meditate on the egg and sperm coming together in a Fantasia-esque symphonic tango. I wanted to relax my body into a state of nirvana, but all I could think of as I lay there was her, Dr. Cornelius. She's either in her office looking at the pictures of herself on the horse or between another set of blotchy white legs, I thought. I wondered why she found babies revolting, why she didn't like me, and why

I felt like a baby. I felt like a despised baby. I thought of my baby who would make all this worth it. I thought about the equestrian center near my house. I wondered whether riding lessons really would be a good esteem builder.

For the next two weeks I waited to feel differently. I've always been very in tune with my body, and I believed I would know immediately when I became pregnant. When I started to feel premenstrual, I figured it hadn't taken. I was right. I got my period a few days later. My hope didn't waver though. I was surprised at that more than anything else. Instead I looked at it as a trial run. It would happen the next time.

Ten

Next Time

*How the magic of "three" may work for comedy
but not for fertility.*

I **THOUGHT** three batches of Viking sperm were more than enough to start my family. It took less than that to populate the state of Minnesota. But they weren't enough. I didn't conceive the next time or the time after that. I was surprised but I thought, "It's not the end of the world. I'll buy more." The good news was that my strained relationship with Dr. Cornelius was better. When she realized that we were both from Chicago, she was instantly nicer. It turned out that she hated her mother, not me.

I went back to the cryobank for more Mr. Right. I took out my credit card as the receptionist accessed my file. I told her I wanted to pick up three more specimens. She said, "I'm sorry, that donor has left the program." I said, "What do you mean?" She said, "We're out of it." If I had wanted to hear that, I could have called Augusta, Georgia. She repeated herself. "It's been discontinued. I'm

69

sorry." "Why didn't you tell me it would run out? I would have ordered more." "We never know when the donor will leave the program," she explained. I just wanted to shake her and yell, "You mean you didn't see it coming? So it's wham, bam, thank-you ma'am in the great big city?" The universe was saying, "Kiss my big galactic ass." The rejection I experienced earlier was nothing compared to the loss and abandonment I felt now.

I was at my lowest point. Over a six-month period I was inseminated four more times. I used a couple of different specimens at the doctor's office that other women had left. The whole fertility business had become a heartless web of donors leaving clients and clients leaving specimens and specimens leaving programs. All sperm looks alike after a while. I was grieving the loss of donor 0780.

Dr. Cornelius began rambling on about more intrusive procedures. Her mad scientist personality dominated our visits now. She lit up when she talked about doing surgery, removing parts that patients no longer needed, then doing practice surgical procedures on those parts after they wheeled the patient into recovery. She told me about some woman's tubes that she had removed. "I mean it was a hysterectomy. Hell, it's not like she'll need them anymore. They're just gonna end up in the dumpster. So I practiced on them. How do you think I became such a good doctor?" She wanted me to get a procedure done to determine whether my tubes were blocked. "It'll hurt a little," she told me.

It was an outpatient procedure. Lisa, my friend and long-time business manager, drove me to the hospital. It's hit and miss determining who's the right person to tag along when you have to go to the hospital. With Lisa I never know which hat she'll be wearing. Would she be the friend I needed and say comforting things to me, or would she be going over my next *Tonight Show* appearance? The last time I went to the hospital, I took a friend who used to be a nurse and was now a comedian. I didn't ask Lisa then because I didn't want to work on my act during surgery. I've heard that's not good for you. It turned out my friend, the ex-nurse, hated ever having been a nurse. She did it to please her mother, and just being in a hospital filled her with rage. So much so that when I expressed feeling discomfort around the incision area and asked her to get a nurse, she told me I didn't need anything for pain and to quit being a baby. It turns out that facilitating someone with their mother issues while undergoing a liver biopsy actually prompted me to go over my next *Tonight Show* appearance. When I told Lisa how mean the ex-nurse had been she gloated, "I should always be the one who goes to the hospital with you. I'm good around sick people; I was raised by a bunch of old women. None of them ever had a good day." She's been going with me ever since.

Dr. Foo looked down the long table at me. He was shorter than Dr. Cornelius so he spoke to me from between my calves. "What did your doctor tell you about this procedure?" "She said it might hurt a little," I told him. "Not might," he said; "it's going to hurt. It 'might' hurt a lot." "Foo" must mean no bullshit. I liked his approach. I wondered whether he had ever taken riding lessons. He gave me some Motrin and explained what he was about to do. He was going to shoot some dye into my uterus and up my tubes. I was going to feel some suction on my cervix and some pressure in my uterine cavity much like very bad cramps. He ended with the mother of all instructions, "Breathe." Whenever anyone has to tell you to breathe, something hideous is about to happen. This was no exception.

I did not breathe. Whatever air was left inside me, I used to swear. I had one tube that wasn't clogged and one that he didn't think was clogged. He said, "Maybe it's spasming because I shot dye into it." I drove home full of self-pity. I love self-pity. I'm both the victim and the spectator. If only I had a castle tower to look out from or a drawbridge to raise. Self-pity is the opiate of feelings. Nothing gets accomplished. How many more strangers would I have to look at between my pale legs to conceive this baby? If I decided to continue, I'd need to get to a tanning bed.

I knew Dr. Cornelius's plan. The procedures would become more and more invasive. I have a very low threshold for pain. I require Novocain to get my teeth cleaned. I used to need pain medicine just to get up in the morning. I am a living example that heroin does lead to chardonnay. I was at another point, but what point was it? I came to this question: how much do I want to force my will onto my body? My life has taught me that it is less painful for me to change myself than to try to change the world around me. But I didn't know what I needed to change.

I had been living with the question How much self-will should I exert? for almost a year. Some questions have to marinate a long time. Some answers come in an instant and you know they're right for you, and some come so slowly, so gradually they just seem like the next thing to do. I asked myself another question: What am I not seeing? And then I saw it, the whole world of babies. I saw all the possibilities of how I might bring a child into my life. After all, it was the love I wanted to experience, not specifically childbirth. I started to look into adoption.

Eleven

Enter Jane

*How my facilitator came from behind enemy lines
to be my best ally.*

I THOUGHT an adoption would take at least five years. I would pursue it as a safety net. It wasn't something that was likely to happen, though, since I was a single woman. In terms of desirability as a prospective adoptive parent, that's one step above incarcerated. In the eyes of the world I was approaching, the world of adoptive families, I was only half of something. In the world of families in general, a single woman is considered half of something. I watched my sister Kathy go through two bad marriages after divorcing the father of her children, in order to escape her less-than feelings about being a single mother. I thought of adoption as a possibility, but I fully believed I would conceive before it became more than plan B.

I was also still hanging on to a fantasy of doing my next *Tonight Show* appearance nine months pregnant. My fantasy went like this: I have finished my set and am sitting with Jay. This is called doing panel in the comedy world. He makes a joke about me bringing a whole new meaning to the term "working mother" and instead of me laughing, my water breaks. He nervously throws to a commercial and I'm ushered into the green room; Kenny G is waiting there and he's told he's going on earlier than planned. I immediately go into labor. I commence to screaming a scream that hasn't been heard since *The Deer Hunter*. I wail through Kenny G's opening number, stopping to catch my breath the moment his song ends. He takes a bow; I take a drink of water and rest. I don't start up again for three minutes, just when he begins a closing arrangement from his new CD now on sale at Starbucks. I give birth before the ambulance gets there, during the commercial break, directly following the show, and name the baby Conan. Not an easy fantasy to let go of.

Around this time my friend Alice, who was also single, had just adopted a baby. She invited me over for a welcoming party. Her baby was a boy, born just a week before. He was beautiful. He was asleep when I got there. I saw that he had ten toes and ten fingers and sweet little camel eyes. We talked as she showed me his nursery. She told me she had used a facilitator to walk her through the entire adoption process. She told me the whole thing took less than a year. That was not what I expected, or wanted, to hear. I couldn't believe how cute she had made his bedroom. My sisters never did anything like that for any of their babies. I had seen rooms like it in movies. I told her how cute the borders around the room were and asked where she had bought them and how much they had cost. I asked because I truly had no idea. It wasn't a matter of whether I could afford it. For all I knew they were painted on and she had done it herself. I thought she probably had done the room herself. She gave me a strange look and said, "What do I care? I'm a millionaire."

I wondered whether that had anything to do with how quickly she had got her baby. I didn't want to ask her any more questions. I was on unfamiliar ground. I knew nothing of millionaire etiquette. The only thing I knew for sure was that I was not a millionaire. If I had known I only had one question, I wouldn't have spent it on the silly circus-animals-in-little-boxcars border. I would have spent it wisely and asked her how much the facilitator cost.

When you struggle with low self-esteem like I some-times do, it can get in the way of success. I often struggled with it in Alice's presence. Alice was always a win-lose situation for me, and she was always the winner. She thought of me as someone with great personal power, therefore I was considered a big kill. I don't believe she thought this on a conscious level. However, you don't get rid of people like Alice. They are an important lesson in life, the lesson being that a problem (in this case self-esteem) lies within yourself. Getting rid of an Alice meant another Alice was just around the corner. There are Alices warming up in the bullpen all over the place.

I wasn't about to leave there empty-handed that day. I held the baby and mingled with others. I had a good time in spite of my rough start. I had more information than I did when I got there, and it changed my thoughts on adoption, single-parent adoption in particular. I put my ego aside and managed to eke out one more question for Alice before I left her and her millions. "Could I get that facilitator's phone number?" Alice was more than happy to give me Jane's number.

I met with Jane at her psychotherapy office in West Hollywood. When Alice told me the adoption facilitator's name was Jane and she was a therapist in West Hollywood, I immediately thought of an old ex-friend who had betrayed me years earlier. She too had had a therapist named Jane in West Hollywood whom she saw on a regular basis. I hadn't thought of that ex-friend in years. I knew the chances of this being the same Jane were not very probable. Still, I was nervous standing at the front door of her office waiting for her to answer.

She opened the door and greeted me warmly. It was the same Jane. I sat down and she began talking. I heard the word "Alice" so I nodded and smiled at her. I don't know what she said during the first few minutes of our meeting. I wasn't listening. Instead I thought of the person who had betrayed me eight years ago, eight years ago when Jane was her therapist, eight years ago when Jane was guiding her through life's little obstacles—like betraying me.

This person shall remain anonymous because merely uttering her name can set off this recurring dream: She and I are standing on a stone wall wearing two-piece bathing suits; it's a breaker wall at the ocean's edge. I'm looking down into the darkest, coldest, most treach-erous water I have ever seen. Sharks would not dare to swim in this water. They were probably across the street at an outdoor café having lunch. So we're on the breaker wall in our swimsuits and she's looking at me and calmly telling me to jump in with her. "C'mon, it'll be fun." I want to jump in with her, but something tells me it won't be as much fun for me as it will be for her. I wake up with the anxiety of a warrior who has fallen asleep in some bushes that are behind enemy lines. It's the feeling of impending doom, of being in a lose-lose situation with no way out. There's no worse feeling for me than this. I get it when something is set in motion that can only end in loss. I can do nothing but watch events unfold until they come to a complete, unpleasant stop of their own accord.

It's the feeling I imagine my father had when his friend got angry, raised a gun, pointed it at him, and squeezed the trigger. He couldn't take the man's anger away. He couldn't stop the bullets from entering his body. His hands couldn't stop them. They passed right through. His connection to God couldn't stop them. He knew the end from the beginning, before the bullet came to a complete stop. That was two months before my fourth birthday. To this day I continue to feel the momentum of that action. I wouldn't know such a feeling of inevitability firsthand for another year, when my family moved into a new house and I met a little neighborhood girl named Joycie.

Two months after my Father died my mother remarried, and moved us all to Florida. She wanted a fresh start. The change would be good for everyone. It would give us kids and also our less-immediate family back in Chicago a chance to adjust to the fact that her new husband was Uncle Jim, my father's brother. I don't know what my sisters and I were expected to adjust to, the death of my father or my mother's new marriage to my uncle. On top of all that, we were in a new climate and knew no one. I adjusted to none of it. I stopped talking. I would talk to my mother and my sisters, but that was it. We stayed in Florida for a year, and then moved back to Chicago.

It was now a little over a year since my father's death. My family moved into a new house. I don't think we were even unpacked yet when one day I stepped out onto the front porch of our new house and spotted Joycie. Looking back, I'm not sure if I stepped out onto my porch so much as I stepped into Joycie's gaze. She lived on the next block, where all the houses were newly built. Her shoes looked new and so did her dress. I imagined Joycie had her own room with a canopied bed. I slept sideways on a double bed with my three sisters. Joycie stood in her front yard staring at me. She stood in the middle of a lush green lawn; sod had been bought and recently rolled out in front of her house for her to walk on. Each blade was perfectly cut the same length, just like her hair. Perfect hair with sharp straight lines. She wasn't like me. I knew looking at her from a distance that she and I would talk differently. She would enunciate like Shirley Temple and other kids on television did. I used words like "git" and "cuz."

I ran a hand over the cowlick in the back of my hair and looked down at our lawn. Tufts of grass and weed held our dog's pooh like a pair of Allstate insurance hands. Our dog, Lady, appreciated a nice lawn; she would meticulously deposit her waste onto the patches of growth like they were plates lined with lettuce and she was catering an event.

Joycie waved me over. (The beginning of an event was set in motion that I felt powerless to stop.) I looked around to make sure it was me she beckoned. She repeated the gesture. I made my way across the street then down the sidewalk until I stood facing her lawn. I thought, oh, if I could have a friend like her I could feel this way all the time. I could feel like I was in a perfect world that didn't need to be fixed. I was enchanted. "Hi, my name is Joycie. Do you want to be in my club?" She didn't ask me what my name was. I said, "Sure," with too much enthusiasm. She looked me over. I expected to go to a clubhouse or at least be shown a secret handshake, but nothing like that happened. She said, "You have to get initiated." That was not what I wanted to hear. My five-year-old mind sensed that things were not above board. The feelings of captivation I had experienced across the street on my porch were fighting to stay alive. My desire to be of value by association was stronger than my intelligence. I looked at the sod she stood on and her ironed clothes and her perfect hair and her new house and I said, "Okay."

The motion of the event was beyond my five-year-old control. She said, "Give me your finger." There was no turning back. I said, "What are you going to do?" She said, "It won't hurt." I slowly extended my finger. I looked at her hands. They were in a hurry. I pulled my finger back and asked, "Who else is in your club?" She smiled and said, "Just me." That was by far the worst news yet. My body felt light as I lifted my hand and gave her my finger. She smiled as she took it in both her hands like a nine iron. She twisted my finger till my arm couldn't follow. Her whole body went under my arm. The pain took my breath away.

It happened so quickly that I don't think I even tried to pull my finger from her grip. I ended up on my knees holding my hurt hand with my good hand and rocking myself back and forth with my breath. I sucked air in and pushed it out until I could regain a sense of my whereabouts. When I got to my feet and looked around she was gone.

It had all happened in what was probably less than a minute. My anger kept me from crying but did not keep the tears from my eyes. I walked up the driveway to a gate while moaning in pain. She was nowhere. Vanished. She must have gone inside the house. I didn't go to the door. Who knew what dangers were behind that? I walked back to my house wounded, angry, and wiser.

The thing I couldn't get a handle on, that I didn't have a word for that day and for a long time afterwards, was betrayal. Today, more than then, I believe that girl was evil. I may have been innocent at five, but I was not a sap. I looked for her every day for a long time, on my way to school and on my way from school. I was going to beat her silly. I looked for her until I wasn't sure what she looked like anymore. I never saw her again. Eventually I wrote her off as someone's visiting cousin.

Twelve

Jane Interrupted

*How things changed
before the ink on Jane's check dried.*

I **THOUGHT** it was best to pass on Jane as my adoption facilitator. Surely I would be better off with someone who hadn't coached an old friend-turned-enemy through the intricacies of betraying me. Then I heard Jane say these magic words: "I have two adopted children." She was glowing. She now had my full attention. She told me her story. By the end, a short ten minutes later, I could see clearly the advantage I would have with her as my facilitator.

She told me that she talks with various adoption agencies on an almost daily basis and guaranteed that both the agency and the state would approve me as a single parent. She would show me how. She had done it for many others like myself, and for herself, a single mother too, not once, but twice, and without so much as one lie. I liked Jane. I thought, "Wow. Jane can make it happen. I think I will go with Jane." Go, Jane, go! See

Jane go! I felt myself glowing just like her. I said, "Well, let's do it." She said, "Great." I said, "How much do you charge?" She said, "That depends on how much you use me." I hate it when people say things like that.

People can be specific about everything but money. I went into a beauty salon in the basement of a casino in Las Vegas once, even though I told myself years before I would never get my hair cut by anyone in a basement. But in Vegas it wasn't so much a basement as it was a part of one big biosphere. Once you enter a casino, they see to it you never have to leave. They provide everything but surgery and a college degree, both of which could be just around the corner. I really needed a haircut so I asked the woman behind the counter how much they charged to cut hair and she said, "Well, it starts at thirty dollars." I said, "I don't want to know where they start. I want to know where they end." She said, "Sixty dollars... depending...."

Did you know that if you stare at someone long enough they will tell you what you need to know? If you're comfortable with long silences like I am you can find out anything. Jane finally said, "It can cost as little as two thousand dollars or up to five thousand, depending on the degree of openness you want in your adoption." I liked Jane a lot. She was already facilitating me and she wasn't even on the payroll yet. I stared some more. She said, "Okay, an open adoption is when you actually meet the birth mother. A closed adoption is when neither of you knows who the other one is. In between there are situations like contact on special occasions or pictures once a year that you agree to send to the birth mother."

What it boiled down to is that the more closed the adoption the more of Jane's services I would need and the more it would cost. Jane would actually go to the delivery room and videotape the birth for a client if they needed her to. She could actually deliver the baby right to your door. I told her I wouldn't require such frills and was leaning more toward a cheaper adoption...I mean an open adoption. I gave Jane a deposit of one thousand dollars.

A week later Jane walked me into the California Adoption Agency. All of the employees said, "Hi, Jane." It was a beautiful thing. Unlike Jane, who had adopted her two children without telling so much as a single lie, I opted for an adoption experience with just one little white lie. I decided it wouldn't be necessary to tell them I was still inseminating. Some may not think

of that as a lie, but I did. It was the lie of omission. I
didn't think they would reject me, but I did think they
wouldn't work as hard for me if they knew.

Deep down inside I knew that my baby was already
on its way. We were moving toward each other. It didn't
matter if we were moving by way of petri dish or by
way of legal paper. It was just a matter of time, time
that I felt I didn't have. My discipline was not to get
too attached to any one means, to stay open to it all—
an alien baby? Why not? If they can abduct, then they
must be able to deliver.

I wanted to get started with a baby. I felt an urgency.
I wanted to speed things up. I wanted to still have an
edge when my baby was born. I figured you probably
lose it around age sixty. If I got started now that would
give me till he's in college with an edge, then I'd pass
the torch to him and some form of my edge would be
carried on. The adoption card was now in the deck. I
could actually relax a little, lay back and put my feet
up so to speak, without seeing Dr. Cornelius between
my legs.

Meanwhile back at the cryobank, new sperm donors
were arriving by the truckload. I was just about to order
some when the most amazing thing happened. I got

a call from Dr. Cornelius. She informed me that one of her patients, who had been using the same donor I had been using, had a couple of specimens left over that she was willing to sell me. Would I like to buy them? "Yes!" I told her. "Wait a minute. Why is she selling it?" "She's pregnant, doesn't need it anymore," Cornelius told me.

I was on an emotional Tilt-A-Whirl. My donor was back. It was a sign from the universe. And now I knew his stuff worked. It was meant to be him all along or why would I have so effortlessly fallen onto more of his sperm? On the other hand, I would now be pretty much buying the stuff on the street. This was a part I could leave out when I told my child his/her story. Then a more frightening thought crept into my conscious-ness: what if I got pregnant from my newly acquired batch of sperm and the already pregnant woman and I lived in the same area? We already went to the same doctor. How many half-siblings might we end up living next door to?

Is anyone keeping an eye on this whole reproduc-tion thing? Who's in charge anyway? I asked a sperm bank professional (I'm not going to mention which sperm bank, but she had a Southern accent). She said,

"You don't have to worry. They only allowed fifty specimens per district." She seemed very satisfied with that
answer, which to me meant she was procreating the
old-fashioned way. I asked, "What's a district?" She
told me she wasn't sure exactly, but she was sure it
was pretty big and "statistically" somethingy something "very unlikely." Let me just paraphrase for you.
Her answer amounted to Nobody's in charge.

Thirteen

The Agency

How The Agency worked its wonder.

I THOUGHT the California Adoption Agency would be an over-lit office full of lawyers in suits with receptionists keeping us wanna-be mothers at bay with fat desks and nail polish. But no. It was like some grass roots organization working for a cause worth fighting for. It was open and casual, yet professional and powerful. It was an intimate setting. Everyone seemed to like each other and like being there. Even though I wasn't sure when I first got there what it was that they did, I was sure they liked doing it. It was contagious. I immediately felt good to be there. Here's what I learned:

The philosophy of the California Adoption Agency (hereafter referred to as The Agency) was to let the birth mother and the adoptive mother pick each other. The Agency was, in essence, a matchmaker. It's an innovative approach as far as adoption is concerned. If you've ever logged onto Match.com, the dating Web site, you know it's not an original concept. The difference between The Agency and Match.com, is The Agency's spiritual aspect.

Everyone at The Agency who works on making a match was at one time a participant in the adoption process. I liked the feeling that gave me. Everyone who was there to guide me through the adoption process had gone before me. More than that, they had gone before me and were sticking around to help me get to where they were. That was the spiritual aspect for me. I think the same spiritual element can be found in Alcoholics Anonymous. It's magical.

The person at The Agency who assisted me in filling out numerous forms was adopted as a child. Another person in charge of files was once a birth mom. The lawyer and his assistant/wife were adoptive parents. The Agency should have been called Adoption World. The people surrounding me were more supportive than I could have imagined. I thought, this must be what gives a new president confidence. They don't have to know how to balance the budget or manage an army. All they have to know is who can. I was learning a valuable lesson. A good parent, like a good president, surrounds herself with good people. I had found Jane, and because of that I was surrounded with people who wanted for me what I wanted for myself... a baby.

Meeting a birth mother had a profound effect on me. I wasn't aware that I had any preconceived ideas of who a birth mother was. I only knew that giving your baby away was an awful thing to do. When I was five, a friend of my dad's brought his five-year-old little girl over to our house and left her there. His wife, the girl's mother, had left them and a newborn baby boy. The little girl lived with us for seven years until her father remarried. Her little brother was taken to a different place to live. I don't think anyone ever came back to get him. Their mother never came back to get either of her kids. My mother never said much about that mother. She would only say that she was a troubled person who didn't want the responsibility of raising kids, didn't want to be tied down; she was wild. The only other thing I knew of birth mothers I learned from the media. A lot of them were crack addicts and alcoholics.

Then I met this woman at The Agency who told me she was a birth mother and said, "If there's anything you want to know about this part of the adoptive experience don't hesitate to ask me." I was struck by her generosity of self. Nothing about her seemed wild. In fact she seemed very centered for such a young person. I guessed she was in her mid twenties. She didn't appear to have a monkey on her back, and I left there and still had my wallet in my purse. She was being of service in the world. For the time being she was in my world, and I was grateful for that. She was lucky. She got to be a part of something that was bigger than her and was having a positive impact on the world.

The last time I got to feel like I was a part of something bigger than me — that I made a difference in the world — was when five other cars and I pulled over to the side of the road to let an ambulance go by. It felt good to be a part of a group effort. It wasn't Habitat for Humanity, but it was teamwork. We don't get together once a year to celebrate. We didn't exchange numbers or even get out of our cars. How pathetic that I'm called upon so infrequently to be of service that I still feel the connection of the five cars that pulled over with me that day.

The Agency explained the match-making process to me. I would write a letter to the birth mother, and they would submit my letter along with other letters to prospective mothers-to-be. I would then wait for one to respond. The adoption thing was getting real pretty fast. They said, "The birth mother letter is perhaps the most important tool in presenting you, the adoptive parent, to your potential birth mother."

The good news for me was that it wasn't an audition. You only get one chance at an audition. My last audition was for an unbalanced character, a crazy person. My acting teacher had recently told me I didn't risk enough. "Don't play it so safe. You'll never get noticed." So I decided to risk it all. The character talked to herself. I decided to put a sock on my hand and talk to a sock puppet instead of to myself. It made me laugh. The producers weren't going to be there. I figured if it was too much, the casting director would tell me to pull in the reins and I'd take the sock off and do the scene. What's the worst that could happen? I wouldn't get the part. Or they would think I was nuts and they'd have something to talk about at dinner that night. At least I'd have fun. I walked into the room, and there were three producers sitting with the casting director. I already had the sock on my hand. The casting director introduced me to them like we were friends. That meant she had faith in me. I committed 100 percent to the sock puppet. She never called me again.

The letter I had to write was something that I could write and rewrite. I told myself what I always tell myself when I have to make a good impression count: at least I didn't have to dance. All I had to do was follow The Agency's simple guidelines:

- Keep the letter brief.

- Describe why you have chosen adoption.

- Describe what you have to offer as a parent. (Readiness, finances, extended family, marriage, experience with children, values and beliefs, what you can give a child: spiritually, emotionally, etc.)

- Describe your home and neighborhood.

- Describe how you play. (Hobbies, interests, and activities.)

- Discuss your career, stressing flexibility in order to care for the child.

- Be yourself.

- Describe yourself in an intimate way.

- Be specific rather than vague.

- Use positive language and avoid dwelling on your history of infertility. (Since I didn't consider myself as having a history of infertility, I substituted "self-loathing" for infertility.)

- When it starts to feel like a chore, put the letter away and come back to it later.

Fourteen

Dear Birth Mother

*How I wrote myself a perfect life
and then realized all of it was true.*

I THOUGHT writing comedy was a challenge. Try writing to a mother to ask her for her baby. It makes the old setup/punch line formula look like a grocery list. I looked at the suggestions and didn't see guidelines at all. I saw a recipe to question my existence. What did I have to give to a child? What have I given anyone so far? I belong to no causes. Causes scare me. I can't think of Sally Struthers without thinking of her asking me for something. I can't remember what she's asking me for, but I know she wants something. And I know she makes me not want to give it to her. It's not humility that makes me uncomfortable. Sally Struthers doesn't come off as humble; she comes off as needy. She seems needier than her cause. I don't think about Jimmy Carter, yet I really admire him. Jimmy Carter shows his humility without seeming needy. I could build low-income houses with him all day long. I wouldn't even need a hammer. Just give me a box of nails. I could just use the heel of my shoe. That's how much I like Jimmy Carter.

I don't identify myself with a race. I don't send birthday cards except to my mother, who for years didn't acknowledge receiving them. I don't keep in touch with anyone from my past. My past being anyone I knew more than eight years ago. I've never been to a high school reunion. I think my school renamed itself after I left, as if to say to the entire graduating class, Don't ever come back. Don't call. Don't even look us up in the phone book. As far as we're concerned, we never laid eyes on one another. We don't exist anymore. Maybe my diploma is no longer good.

The only suggested guideline that sounded surmountable was "keep your letter brief." That meant leave them wanting more. That would be easy for me. Brevity is my specialty. One of my favorite Shakespearean scenes is in *King Lear.* King Lear asks his three daughters to profess their love for him and in return he will reward them with his kingdom. The first two daughters go on and on about how much they love him. The third daughter, Cordelia, who really loves him most, refuses to answer him. He's embarrassed in front of his servants. He becomes furious and tells her to answer, "What have you to say?" "Nothing," Cordelia says. He screams at her, "Nothing will come of nothing!" Nothing may very well come of nothing, but a lot can come from little. That's how I feel about brevity. It's powerful, and on some irrational level I think less can go wrong.

How does one measure a life in progress? I must be doing something. I'm always busy. Then it dawned on me. I pay my mortgage. My mortgage is the reason for everything I do. So many times I've wanted to quit working, quite writing, quit getting up in the morning, but I told myself, "You have to go on; you have a mortgage. Get up. Put on some pants; you have a mortgage." I write jokes for the mortgage, return phone calls for it, get on airplanes for it, and have my picture taken for it. I go out on stage and make people laugh so they can forget for a moment that they have a mortgage.

My friend Lisa thought I was being too hard on myself. She reminded me, "You recycle." How could I have forgotten? I guess you really can't see the forest for the trees. I am an environmentalist. Not a big plus for getting a baby, but it was a relief to know I'm doing something good in the world. I take pride in my recycling and my ability to waste nothing.

Their last suggestion came in handy. "When it starts to feel like a chore, put the letter away and come back to it later." I put the suggestions away immediately and came back to them later. Over and over I put them away. I couldn't see that my letter would add up to much. I had never even written a resume. My resume was nothing more than my film and television credits, and they didn't apply to the job of being a mother. I was asking for so much. I was asking someone to entrust me with the job of being a mother to their child. I felt entitled to be a mother, but did I deserve to be given a baby? I had the humility to write the letter, but feeling entitled to what I wanted wasn't always at my fingertips. I had to fight for it just as I had as a child.

When I was growing up, my sisters and I would complain to our mother that our stepfather had hit us. We wanted her to tell us that we didn't deserve to be hit, that we were entitled to be treated with respect. But that's not what she told us. She would tell us, "Oh, you kids act like you're abused. You don't know what it's like to be abused. I just read in the paper last week about some parents that held their kid's hands over the stove and burned them. That's abuse. Your father just overreacts." It's not a story I would ever include in my letter, but it is part of what I had to overcome on my journey to motherhood.

One day after telling my therapist, Susan, about a particular beating by my stepfather she asked me, "Where was your mother?" It was one of those rare questions that feel like a shot of espresso in my system. It made me spin inside. I had never thought to wonder where she was. Like those stick-on pieces of a picture I played with when I was little, I didn't have the smiling mother to stick on my picture of abuse. I told Susan I didn't know. I don't remember ever seeing my mother there when he hit us. He must have done it when she wasn't around. She was probably sleeping or in another room or at work.

The last time he hit me was my senior year in high school. He tore the sleeve out of my coat and threw me on the ground and kicked me, calling me names. All I could do was cover my face with my arms and curl up like an armadillo. I didn't move of my own accord until he stopped kicking and ordered me, "Get out of my sight." I couldn't move my ribs for over a week. When I told my mother what he did and that I couldn't bend my side she said, "You deserved it." That's where she had been all those years. She had been the invisible voice saying, "You deserve it." I never trusted her again. I would never again think of her as someone who was wise and intelligent, as someone I could look up to. I also knew from that single exchange with my mother that she had no idea who I was. She did not know that I deserved to be treated as someone of value and that I was entitled to all the good that the world contained.

I had to write the letter or I'd be an invisible voice saying, "I don't deserve to be a mother." I don't dwell on my past, but it's a useful tool to me. I like that I have access to my past but I'm no longer stuck there. I had done the work of unsticking for over ten years. I had taken apart the life I was stuck in and put back together a life that was full of hope. I was free to roam back and forth between the two. When something feels bad to me, it usually means I'm revisiting my past. Sometimes that's necessary in order to move forward. I use this prayer to help me when I forget my way home: I am no longer a victim of my past, nor do I fear the future. I live in the present surrounded by God's love.

I took one break after another, but I wrote my letter. The most challenging part was the restraint and awareness it took not to say anything unappealing about me, my family, my outlook, and my neighborhood — about anything. So I mentioned that I live near a beautiful park, not that I drive by graffiti to get there. I said I run and play with my dog, Molly, in the park and left out the part about the Hillside Strangler dumping bodies on the trail years earlier.

Writing the letter was an exercise in affirmations. What I ended up with was the most positive presentation of myself, my life, and my world that I had ever put forth. I read my letter and wanted that lady to adopt me. And it was all true. It was me without all the negatives hovering above my shoulders. It was my life observed by my higher self.

Fifteen

Cheeeeese!

How every picture tells a story.

I **THOUGHT** a trunkful of family photographs would render at least one appropriate picture to tape to my birth mother letter. The Agency suggested I include a couple of pictures of me with other people that conveyed a message of love and friendship. They suggested that the pictures have kids in them and added, "Dogs are always good." A dog wasn't the hard part for me. I had the best dog in the world. She was rotten to the core like a dog should be. She was petted to sleep every night on my lap. I knew I'd have to dig deep for a family picture conveying love and friendship so I set an entire night aside. Compared to writing the letter choosing a snapshot would be easy.

I went through an entire box of pictures of me with my family. None of them conveyed love and friendship; they conveyed separateness and obesity and depression. Every picture taken at my mother's house had too much clutter in it. Not new clutter such as grocery bags to be emptied. That would indicate prosperity. No, this was old dusty clutter that said, "Too many garage sales, not enough garage space." Maybe Jane could have some of the mess airbrushed out. My mother's antique doll collection in the background looked like a Chuckie convention. None of the people in any of the pictures were looking at each other. In some shots there was laughing, but you got the feeling they were each hearing a different joke.

I spent hours looking at photos. I could not remove myself. It was a much overdue trip down memory lane. But as far as serving my immediate needs, it was an exercise in futility. Nostalgia was coursing through my veins and paralyzing me. I was underwater with a dozen jellyfish who were innocently playing a game of sting the lady. It all made me homesick. I knew as I neared the bottom of the box that I couldn't use any of the pictures. I needed different images, images that conveyed love. The Agency said outdoor scenes would be best for the pictures. They were right. That's why they're The Agency. There was light outdoors and nothing but possibilities—and no clutter.

I decided I would get some friends together, go in my back yard, and shoot a roll. That turned out to be a very short-lived idea. I realized that no one I know well enough to ask to be in some pictures with me had kids. The Agency said I needed kids in the pictures. My life as it was could not provide such pictures. It was settled. I would have to borrow photos from someone else's life. If I wanted to create a pictorial essay on a life filled with kids and love and friendship, I'd have to go with strangers.

I was working in Nashville at the time. Do you know the good thing about Nashville? It's full of strangers. I won't mention the name of the club I was performing at because they never paid me well enough to promote them. I enlisted one of the local comedians I had met the night before to drive me to a park Saturday morning and take some pictures. She happened to be a photographer. I told her my plan, how we had to find a happy family on an outing and blend in with them. She was enthusiastic, even mentioned the movie *Zelig*.

We got to the park early. I couldn't believe my luck. There were kids everywhere. So this is where they're hiding, I thought. Things hadn't changed at all. The local park was where I went as a kid. I spent most of my time there either ice skating or playing softball. Something was different here, though. But what was it? The park was nicer, more colorful; plastic and wood structures, not rusty metal like when I was a kid. I was having a hard time blending. Parents were staying very close to their kids. That's when I realized what the real difference was. There were parents there. They were everywhere. They were swarming the place. Some were even on bikes. When did parents start going to the park?

The only memory I have of either of my parents going to the park is when my dad went there to vote on election day. No one's parents went to the park or rode a bike when I was a kid. If a grown-up rode a bike in the park when I was a kid, it meant they were retarded, or, as we used to say then, touched in the head. It wasn't written anywhere, but it was the rule. When you got to be a certain age, you just didn't go to the park or ride bikes anymore. Your stomach got big and you either stood or sat. I remember grown-ups looked uncomfortable to be up off their feet. They didn't swim much either. They would water ski, but that was because they had something to stand on; they were still on their feet. And even if they fell, they were on their ass, their other position of comfort. On your feet or on your ass was the rule for grown-ups.

I couldn't believe how closely parents were watching their kids. What had the world come to? You couldn't even pick up a stray ball and try to jump in a game of soccer with some four-year-olds anymore without creating a stir. How would I ever blend in enough to take some snapshots with these kids? I knew if I tried to take a picture, I would be driven back with sticks and held for the police. I started to feel like a criminal, like I was doing something wrong.

In theory it had seemed reasonable to take pictures with strangers but once there among the children I knew that I was treading on sacred ground. It would be a sin for me to take a child's image without their parent's permission. I had to come clean with the parents or I wouldn't get the pictures I desperately needed to complete my birth mother letter.

Why is it so hard to tell the truth when it matters so much? It's easy when I have nothing to lose, so easy I don't even know I'm telling the truth. It's as easy as talking. But if I think I might lose something I have or not get something I want, it's really tough.

My higher self tells me the universe will effortlessly support an act that is in harmony with what is good. That day my lower self doubted the universe would be as supportive if a mother was around. So I walked over to a father alone with his two beautiful blond-haired, blue-eyed children and told him a very abbreviated version of my story. He not only believed me, he was more than happy to help me. He energetically joined my mission. He welcomed the sense of adventure and generously loaned me his two kids for my birth mother letter. He seemed equally glad that their mother wasn't there. He put the girl in my arms and the boy on my knee. The Friday night comedian went click, click, click, and presto I had the pictures I needed, pictures that conveyed love and friendship. I will never forget the kind father who helped me become a mother.

Sixteen

Sitting Pretty

*How having all my ducks in a row
gave me the two-baby crazies.*

I THOUGHT my work was done and all I had to do was sit back and enjoy the ride. My birth mother hook was baited and out there working its magic, and Jane was in the crow's nest. I had a couple batches of sperm on ice, and a new ovulation kit in the cabinet. My baby net was widening.

It didn't occur to me that I should worry until the next time I was inseminated. I was on the table. Dr. Cornelius had finished with me and was in the next room thawing another batch for her next client. I was resting at a comfortable incline so the sperm could run downhill. Cornelius wasn't as cheery next door now as she once was. She stayed with me longer and talked. I made her laugh. I was now her pet.

In my own way, unbeknownst to her, I was trying to help her forgive her mother for not being a nice person. "She's just a mean, unhappy woman who wants

111

everyone around her to suffer," said Cornelius. I told her that her mother sounded afraid. Cornelius, on the other hand, was afraid of nothing, a warrior with the ability to create life. "She's not afraid. What's she afraid of?" I said, "Everything... the world she lives in." Cornelius assured me, "She's just a bitch." She said it like it was a scientific fact. Like I should abandon my research immediately and refer directly to her folders full of data about her mother. If her mother had been an unexplored frontier, I knew Cornelius would have become excited like she did when she talked about mastering surgical techniques. She didn't get excited, and I knew better than to argue with science. Her mother would remain a bitch until Dr. Cornelius said otherwise. However, the seed of forgiveness had been planted. I didn't need to stand around with a hose and waste water.

It always staggers me when I hear someone call their mother a bitch. I always think, Wow, what went on between them that made this person feel so strongly about their own mother? And my next thought is always, what kind of bitch was that mother that her own child thinks she's a bitch? It's one thing when you're thought of as a bitch at work or by your mechanic or even at the department store where you shop. But when it's your daughter or your son you can be sure it's also your dry cleaner and fellow parishioners. When I think "bitch," I think "evil." My mother was many things, but never evil. And she was never afraid of the world around her. It was the world inside her that she feared. The external world was manageable. She even welcomed the world beyond, you know, the world on the other side.

My mother wasn't evil unless you think contacting the dead is evil. She used to have her friends over as a group for two events: Bunco, which is a dice game, and séances to try to reach people on the other side. If no one she knew was available on the other side to communicate with her, she would just get information on the living. Who gave her the information is anyone's guess. I'll have to ask her. Both occasions brought forth bowls of bridge mix and gelatin orange slices and mint leaves coated in sugar. That particular candy meant she was having a special evening with her girlfriends. It was the only time those candies were ever in our house.

I loved those occasions. They were exciting. From around corners and crouched at table legs, I watched my mother interact with her friends. It was her personal time, a rarity, and all kids were to be scarce.

The women laughed loud and often, smoked cigarettes, and ate candy. Some of them even swore. Swearing wasn't allowed in our house except when my stepfather got really mad. Then it was only God damn it, son of a bitch, and what the hell.

My very first swear word was "f----r." A kid on a bicycle with a banana seat and high handlebars rode past me doing about thirty miles per hour. The handlebar caught me in the gut, and out came "F----r." I was eight. No one was with me, yet I felt my world, in the span of a single spoken word, had changed. It was a psychic glimpse into the future. It was who I would become for a while. Would my mother, the omniscient one, get wind of it during one of her séances? Not that she needed a séance to connect with her psychic powers. She didn't. I saw her as a full-time psychic. Would my child see me as all knowing? I hoped not.

I will never forget one particular séance that my mother conducted. I was supposed to be in bed, but who can sleep when her mother is downstairs talking with the dead? I sat on the staircase looking down into the living room. Candles were lit, and my mother and her friends sat around a card table with joined hands. My mother didn't speak in the requisite wispy voice to reach the other side. She spoke in her regular voice, the one she used when she meant business, when she ordered me, "Get in there and get those dishes done."

She spoke to the darkness, "George...if you're in the room let us know. Give us a sign." It was my father she was talking to. I had never heard my mother speak his name. "George, please give us a sign." The candles flickered. Was he in the room? I knew if anyone could make it back, it would be him. He was that strong. All of a sudden the front door swung open and in barged my stepfather, drunk. She had asked for George's spirit and instead had gotten his brother, intoxicated with Seagram's spirits, and he was not happy. "What the hell is going on here? Christ sakes, what are you doing in here with all these candles?" Everyone let go of the hands they were holding. He flipped on a light. "Are you out of your mind? I told you to stop this shit."

It wasn't the last séance my mother held, but it was the one that told me my father was never coming back in any form. And if he was out there at all, why would he let someone like my stepfather, who scared me so much, live with us? My mother wasn't afraid of him, just my sisters and me and Lady, our dog. We were the ones he hit. My mother's last séance occurred soon after that. She used astrologic charts to predict that her friend's mother would die soon, and shortly thereafter the woman died. My mother didn't want that kind of power, so whatever she knew about the other side, she no longer shared it with anyone.

Dr. Cornelius's mother had made her mad enough to get a medical degree. Cornelius had risen above where she came from to a place where she could enjoy her anger. Anger travels well and is only enjoyable when you're successful. To stay where you came from and be angry is tragic. Dr. Cornelius was not a tragic person; she was a good doctor. I had a feeling this insemination was going to work. "The third time's a charm," she said as she stepped on a pedal under the table. I began my descent. That's when it hit me that I had a lot more to worry about than Dr. Cornelius's relationship with her mother.

What if the adoption agency called with a baby and I took it home and four weeks later I realized I was pregnant? My downward spiral went like this: how will I deal with two kids? I'm single. I'll have to get an abortion. I can't get an abortion. I'm forty. Me sitting at an abortion clinic with fifteen-year-olds? They'll think I'm someone's mother. I'll have to keep both babies.

I hope I won't favor the birth child over the adopted one. I can hear me now telling the nanny, "I'm gonna take the baby for a walk, you stay here and watch the Romanian." My lower self was at it again. I spent the next four weeks in and out of the two-baby crazies.

Seventeen

Social Services

How I fell short and then my therapist
cleared my name with the normal police.

I THOUGHT I was perfectly normal until the nice lady from Los Angeles County Social Services paid me a visit. She had a briefcase. I kept staring at it resting against my couch. The only time a briefcase had ever been in my house was the time I refinanced. His was nice with a lot of positive energy. Hers was worn. Hers was upsetting. Hers worked for the county.

The Agency told me a person from Social Services was coming to do a home study, and I should keep my answers short and pleasant. I didn't see any harm in offering the woman a glass of water. She seemed parched. Not parched from a single day but from a lifetime of not enough water. She had the demeanor of someone who'd handled too many forms in her life. I knew we were two different species. I was sure she slept in a filing cabinet. The only thing I thought we might have in common was tea. But I wasn't about to say, "I bet you're a tea drinker, aren't you?" That wouldn't be keeping it short, and I was supposed to keep it short. If she didn't like me, I wouldn't get a baby. She had all the power. I knew that the more I revealed, the greater my chances were of saying the wrong thing.

I'm not a person who sits around and wonders, Am I normal? I can't even bring myself to put quotation marks around the word. Now I know how all those gorillas felt in the mist when Diane Fosse showed up. They didn't know she was Diane Fosse. They thought she was a poacher whom they might have to disarm. She showed up in their world and started taking notes.

I had a woman in my world with a briefcase full of notes. All I could think was, how does my world look to her? If you live in a barn with horses, you can't smell the horse manure. I'd been in my world so long I couldn't smell it anymore. But she could. She could smell my flaws, my secrets, my fear, and the musty sponge on the kitchen sink. She wasn't afraid of me. She was drinking the water I'd given her. I'm a person who won't even read my reviews for fear of empowering others with the ability to determine my worth, and now all of a sudden someone else's opinion mattered. I cared about the review this lady was there to give me.

She asked me if I thought I would get married one day. Her nosiness made me mad. I wanted to say, "I'm sure if I do decide to get married it will be one day. I hope it doesn't take any longer than that." I didn't say that though. I thought it was an odd question and wondered if my mother had put her up to it. Apparently she was there to examine me, my life, and my world. She wasn't just there to determine whether I would make a good mother. She was there to find out why I wasn't a good wife; I was sure of it. She must be looking for evidence of some sort, asking herself, "Why hasn't anyone married this woman? Why is she looking for a baby when she should be out looking for a husband?"

I said, "If I waited for the right person to come into my life to do the things I want to do, I'd still be waiting to get cable." When cable first came into being, I waited over four years for the right person to come into my life so we could split the cost. Back then I didn't go to the movies alone either. I told her I don't wait for anyone. I'm here to live a life, not wait for one. The pieces of my life haven't fallen together the way I was told they were supposed to. If I still believed in that old template, I would still be waiting to buy my first house, I'd still be waiting to start a family, and I'm sure I'd still be waiting for the social worker to leave.

When I have overwhelming feelings, I move my body. I don't eat like a lot of people do when they have strong feelings. I vacuum when I'm upset and scrub floors on my hands and knees. It doesn't matter whose house I'm at, either. If you want your house cleaned, invite me over and then upset me.

I asked her if she'd like to see the house. Boy, would she. She went all over my house, asking questions about my personal life as we moved from room to room. We got to the back of the house where a bedroom was set up. "Who lives here with you?" she asked. I said, "Denise, a friend from Chicago." "I wasn't aware that you had someone else living here with you." That's what she said. What I heard was, "You've just made the biggest mistake of your life. And I'm sure it's just the tip of the iceberg. What else are you hiding? Anne Frank is in the attic isn't she? Don't you worry, my little pretty, I'll find out everything." It isn't what she said, it's just what went racing through me. I explained how Denise had moved to Los Angeles six months ago and was an aspiring editor who would be staying with me until she got on her feet. She said, "I'll give you a form for her to fill out. She'll have to be fingerprinted." "Okay." I opened the door and led her into the backyard.

She admired my organic tomato garden. I knew she would. The caged plants were flush with fruit and towered over her. All I could think was, how do I tell Denise she has to get fingerprinted? I knew one thing. I'd have to wait at least another month before I could raise the rent. You can't ask someone to get fingerprinted on your behalf then ask them to pay more rent that same month. I asked, "Why do you need Denise's fingerprints?" She said, "We have to make sure she doesn't have a felony record. We won't place a child in a home with someone who's been convicted of a sex crime or is a known pedophile." Denise was the opposite of a sexual predator if I ever saw one. I doubted whether she had even had sex before. She was twenty-two, a shy person, and she apologized too much.

When I first met Denise in Chicago, I asked her where she was from. She said she grew up in Michigan. When I asked what part of Michigan, she used her hand as a visual aid. She held it up as if it had a mitten on it. "This is Michigan." She drew an invisible circle around her mittened hand. She pointed to the spot where her thumb curved into her palm and said, "Okay, this is Detroit and I'm from right over here." She pointed to the crease where her index finger met her palm. I asked, "Do people in Italy do that with their feet?" She laughed like it was the funniest thing she'd ever heard. I believe it may have been.

Before we went back inside I offered the Social Services lady a few tomatoes to take with her. It was my Midwestern way of saying good-bye. I closed the door behind us and turned to lead her back into the living room where I hoped her briefcase would be waiting at the door for her. She wasn't from the Midwest so she didn't leave. Instead, she lingered at the foot of Denise's bed, looked up at me, and said, "I hope you're telling me the truth about your relationship with Denise. You know, we except a lot more now than we used to." My heart was in my throat. This was one of those times when I was glad I'm a performer. I said, "Of course I'm telling you the truth about Denise." I said it as if her concern was the silliest thing I'd ever heard. On some level it was. The main thing was that I didn't show the fear that was making its way back down my throat into my chest.

Apparently her briefcase wasn't from the Midwest either because it wasn't at the front door ready to leave. It was leaning against the couch right where she'd left it. She sat down next to it and removed my file. She looked it over and started asking me questions about my family. The file contained my "yes/no" answers on numerous forms. Apparently they weren't colorful enough for this lady's curiosity so we sat and talked about my family for a while. I considered myself an expert on them because I had been talking about them in therapy for over eleven years. All I had to do was put a positive spin on the truth, a skill I had learned from my therapist, a gift I had acquired over the years. My higher self assures me there is a gift in every encounter. My lower self considers it a challenge to stay open to receive a gift. It's getting easier. My lower self doesn't get in the way of the gifts as often as it used to.

She asked me about being in therapy like it was a strange and rare occurrence. Maybe I had lived in New York too long, but I was operating under the assumption that if your mother was Jewish or you were Jewish or if you knew or lived near a Jewish person, you had the right to a therapist. I didn't think it would warrant attention when I put "yes" next to that question in the mental health section of the adoption application. "We're going to need to know why you were in therapy. If you could fill this out at your earliest convenience." I had never been asked to articulate why I was in therapy so I wasn't sure how to respond when she handed me yet another form to fill out. Let me offer these words to the unwise. If a "yes" answer will generate more forms to fill out, do what our First Lady Nancy Reagan told us to do, "Just say no."

My stomach was growling. It was almost dinnertime. The lady had just about accused me of lying about my roommate, Denise, and had slapped another form on me to fill out that would divulge even more of my not-so-private-anymore life. "I should let you know a similar form will be sent to your therapist," she said. Then she did something that totally caught me off guard. She began asking me questions about my friend Alice, whom I'd mentioned on one of the forms as the person who had referred me to The Agency. Alice was very famous and had absolutely nothing to do with my adoption process. The Social Services lady wanted to know how long I'd known her, where we had met, what she was doing now, had I seen her baby, et cetera. The lady was genuinely excited. I was genuinely concerned. What did it have to do with my adoption?

The answer, I found out later, was that it had nothing to do with my adoption. My lawyer told me that her behavior was unprofessional and self-indulgent. He couldn't believe how long she had stayed and claimed he had never heard of a home study taking close to five hours. "An hour, an hour and a half is common. This was some personal agenda of hers," he said. He made it clear to me, though, that it would do little good to bring up any Los Angeles Social Services personnel on misconduct because they are seldom reprimanded and never dismissed. "Once they get the job, they have it for life," he said. "It's best not to rock the boat too much even though from where I sit her conduct was a blatant abuse of power." He didn't think it was in our best interest to file a formal complaint, but he would mention it to her supervisor. It never came up again.

Susan got her letter from Social Services and filled it out in the briefest way possible. I was in therapy to deal with the death of my father. That's also all I wrote on my form. It was true. I'd never thought of it so simply. He died, my mother swept it under a rug, and I remained broken until I dealt with that loss.

Eighteen

Nibbles

*How I found my limitations
and discovered they were defined not only by me,
but also by my family.*

I THOUGHT a little African American baby boy born
on Martin Luther King's birthday not only would be
beautiful but could very well be president of the United
States some day. When Jane called to tell me a baby
was just born whom I could get, I was ecstatic...for
about one minute. Then I thought of my mother, who
was not only artistic (she painted ceramics for years)
but who for many years had been involved in racist
activities. Her group wasn't organized enough to be a
militia. They were for the most part nonviolent. They
didn't go looking for trouble. They were more separatist
than anything else. Their weapons were petitions and
picket signs, the latter of which, unfortunately, can be
used as actual weapons.

Jane's adopted kids were both African American.
And both came from the same birth parents. She made

it look so easy. They don't get any whiter than Jane. Blond hair, blue eyes, flat ass. She was a great mother and went out of her way to bring African culture into her children's lives. She drove many extra miles so they could go to a racially mixed school. I was sure I wouldn't have to drive as far as her. She lived closer to the beach than I did.

African American culture resonated with Jane. She was at home with it. When I filled out the questionnaire at The Agency, I was asked what "racial range" I would consider. I put Caucasian or Hispanic. I thought I had enough on my plate being a single parent. I didn't think I had it in me to learn and teach another culture. Jane told me she was aware of my racial range but thought she'd present the child to me anyway. Her instincts were right. I did get excited. A baby was a baby was a baby, and I had nothing but love to give. After all, my prayer had been to have a child who would get just as much from me as I would from them. I asked Jane for a little time. She gave me just that . . . a few hours. I wanted to call my mother. What would she think? Had she evolved in twenty-six years?

Twenty-six years ago in 1968, I was an eighth grader at Mount Greenwood Elementary school on the south side of Chicago. Aside from what I saw on the five o'clock news, I led a very sheltered existence. I knew nothing of ethnicities. There were a lot of Irish and even more Catholics in my neighborhood. Everyone had the same nose. My mother was Russian Jew and French but looked like everyone else. The only noticeable difference was that she didn't go to church with us on Sundays. One day I asked her why and she said, "Because I already know right from wrong. Church is for people who don't know the difference. I want you to know the difference." It made total sense to me. My stepfather swore and drank and lied. My mother did not. When a boy would call who I didn't want to talk to, I'd tell my mother to tell him I wasn't home. She would hand me the phone and say, "Don't ever ask someone else to do your lying for you."

My stepfather, in the same situation, was eager to lie for me. He would tell the guy, "I'm not sure if she's here. Let me check." Then he'd ask me, "Are you here? It's Warren." I would shake my head, and he'd get back on and say, "Yeah, Warren? She's not here, man. She must be out with her friends. I'll try to remember to tell her you called, man. I usually remember. I might forget once...twice a day, tops. Sure, you can call back later, as long as it's not after dark. Okay, man. Bye, man." My stepdad only used the word "man" when he dealt with our boyfriends. He enjoyed lying for my sisters or me. He turned it into a performance for us. He also still went to church. But not every Sunday and not all holidays. His churchgoing was sporadic at best.

Desegregation was a big issue back in the '60s. The civil rights movement, in some form, was on the news every night. The gay marriage issue of today pales in comparison to the heat the civil rights movement created. There was movement every day. Martin Luther King was a great leader. Even my stepfather admired him, though he would never say it with words. He would recite parts of King's speeches. He felt threatened by Dr. King like most of the people in my young, white world did, but he also realized King was a great man, a man who should be listened to. My stepfather was racist but argued with it inside himself. One day he said to me, "If they weren't black, how would we know who to hate?" My mother never gave King any credit.

On Halloween my mother dressed my sisters and me up as African Americans. She would burn the end of a cork, let it cool, then color our faces and necks and hands with it. Then she'd put red bandannas on our heads and send us out trick-or-treating. People would give us candy and laugh at us. Some of them would call to their husbands, "Honey, come and look. It's four little Aunt Jemimas." My mother thought it was funny. We just wanted candy.

My neighborhood as a whole was very racist. It was one of the few all-white neighborhoods left in Chicago. Civil servants were required to live within the boundaries of the city, and a lot of policemen and firemen lived in my neighborhood. My school was chosen as one of the all-white schools to participate in busing, which was met with violent opposition. White people began protesting and picketing. They came from other neighborhoods with signs that said, "Go home!" or "Over my dead body." We lived across the street from the school and had a bird's-eye view of the activity. My stepfather forbade my mother to picket, so she did the next-best thing. She offered our house as a coffee-and-donut rest stop for the anti-busing demonstrators who circled the school.

Through my window I could see friends of my mother, the ones who came to her séances, picketing down below. From my classroom seat, I could see the big homemade signs they had made and nailed to wooden boards. They would jeer at the children being escorted into the building when they arrived in the morning and again as they were escorted back onto the bus after school. They would also yell and scream at the pro-busing people. There weren't many of them, maybe four. My mother stopped letting the protesters use our house as a pit stop the day her good friend Ann Wheat was hauled off to jail for clobbering a pro-busing guy over the head with her picket sign.

But that was years ago. My mother had surely changed since then. The whole world had changed. When I called her, my nephew Tommy answered the phone. He hadn't been happy to hear my voice since having visited me in California. I had had to ask him to leave because he was shooting up crystal meth in my bathroom. I was the cool aunt until then. He quickly handed my mother the phone. I heard him say, "It's Peggy." I told my mother, "They called and offered me a baby!" She said, "When?" I said, "Today, just now. He was just born." She said, "Where?" I said, "In California; I think in L.A. His mother is African American." She said, "So the baby's black?" I said, "Well, I'm not sure what the father is." She didn't say anything. I wasn't sure what else to say.

I thought she had changed when my little brother was hit by a car twenty years earlier. It happened while they were on vacation in Florida. He was crossing a street with my brother Jimmy when a speeding car sent him into the air. Jimmy picked him up and hid him in some bushes, and then ran and got my parents. The doctors told my mother they weren't sure whether he would live. My mother spent the next six months in a Florida hospital with him. Other mothers, many of them African American, were also nursing their kids back to life from terrible accidents. Automobile wrecks, gunshot wounds, some of them self-inflicted, falls, and dives had left their children paralyzed. The mothers, both black and white, were all in the same boat. Some of their kids made it, and some didn't. My mother saw the suffering they all had in common. These women supported each other. They supported my mother. They opened her and filled her with hope. They changed her.

Finally she said, "I know you really want this baby. I think if you could just wait, another one will come along." I could hear my nephew laughing in the background. I heard him say, "Oh man, is she gonna adopt a shine, Grandma?"

I got off the phone immediately. When I feel anger rise up inside me like the fire of an incinerator, I move away from the source. Nothing good ever came from seeing those feelings through. It's tempting to fight the fight when my lower self is beckoned by someone else's lower self. Stoking that fire with the sweetness of self-righteousness is way too much energy for my body to hold. I get sick from that much activity because I have the adrenal glands of a large athletic man. I have to be careful. If I'm not mindful of self-righteousness, I could wake up to find myself marching with some religious group.

I called Susan and told her what had happened. I told her I didn't know what to do. She said, "You have to ask yourself how you want your adoption to feel and follow that." How did I want it to feel? I never thought it would really happen. Now that it might, I wanted it to feel like the best, most sacred day of my life. The way having a baby should feel. I wanted to feel blessed and happy beyond reason.

My mother didn't do anything wrong. She didn't regress into her old racism, and she didn't reconnect with the spirit of her African American sisters back in Florida. She even emitted sensitivity. It was my nephew's laughter that I kept hearing. Like it or not, my family would also be receiving this baby. How could I bring a baby into such a challenging world and not provide him with a home base of unconditional love? Even if my mother loved him, I would still be bringing him into an atmosphere of judgment.

The most telling of the questions I asked myself before calling Jane back was, "Couldn't I go meet the baby?" I thought that if he was light like Denzel Washington I would take him home. If he was dark like Bigger Thomas, I could always say no. I hadn't even met the baby and my love had become conditional. I called Jane and told her I couldn't take that beautiful little baby. Jane called me later that day and told me a couple who had been waiting a long time took the baby boy. They were on cloud nine. What a perfect world we'd live in if we could all be raised by parents who had waited a long time for us and wanted us more than anything.

Nineteen

An Active Mind Is the Devil's Workshop

How my views on teen pregnancy changed.
I'm for it. (Slap.) No, I'm against it. (Slap, slap.)
I'm for it and against it.

I THOUGHT it would take two years or a computer glitch for my name to come up again on the adoption waiting list. Two months went by before I heard back from Jane. This time it was a Malaysian baby who had been promised to a Chinese couple who were now hesitating. The birth mother was Malaysian, and the birth father was Pakistani. "The woman is hesitating," Jane told me. "I'm just preparing a backup plan if they back out. I'll know in the next two hours." I said, "Okay." She said, "Don't get too attached. It may or may not happen. Think about it. I'll call you back." I said, "Okay." That was the entire conversation.

To hear myself confess this makes me cringe: for the next two hours I called everyone I knew and went on the

Internet trying to find out what a Malaysian baby was. You can't just punch "Malaysian baby" into the keypad on Google and get a picture of a Malaysian newborn. You're more apt to get a massage parlor. I considered myself to be well traveled before the adoption process. I had lived in New York for eight years. I knew what Pakistani people looked like. But I didn't know anything about Malaysians. I needed to be able to picture this baby I was being told was available. This could be my child. It had to be love at first sight. I needed to visualize him and then immediately want to put my arms around him.

Someone, I forget who, I must have blocked it out, told me, "Malaysian is like Hawaiian." I said, "I thought that was Polynesian." They said, "It's both. It's Malaysian, Indonesian, Polynesian; there's not that much difference." I had my doubts; fears really, so I went right into judgment mode. I tell you, my lower self is busier than the president. Downward spiral 2365: "How can they think all these ethnic groups look the same? They probably don't see the difference between a person of Chinese, Japanese, or Korean descent. Why am I surprised? They're so insensitive, they probably don't taste the food they eat or know their pants are too tight either."

Jane called within an hour to tell me the adoptive mother was taking the baby after all, that she didn't know what she had been thinking, she desperately wanted that baby. Happy endings are what Jane specializes in.

All I could think was, "Where's my happy ending?" There is nothing I enjoy more than justifiable self-pity. I recommend it. Just try to have the wherewithal not to take self-pity too seriously. I consider having difficulty starting a family a high-end problem. If you're disease free, not addicted to drugs, tobacco, or alcohol, have a job, and own a home, your problems are high-end problems. People don't line up around the block to feel sorry for you. Unless you got stuck in a well trying to start a family . . . that's another story. After you explained why you were in the well naked the whole country would be rooting for you. If you're trying to get off of skid row and you show up for your counseling appointments on time, the government will feel sorry for you and get you teeth and a place to live and help you find a new career. A single woman trying to adopt a baby, all she has at her disposal is self-pity . . . and Jane, thank God.

Jane checked in with me every other week for the next two months. During that time The agency called and asked me to add something to my letter. They told me I might experience more activity if I let the birth mother know I empathized with her. So I added empathy to my letter. I wrote that I would always speak highly of her to the child. It's hard to write to someone whom you know nothing about. Was I writing to a woman or a teenager? The only thing I knew for sure that all birth mothers considering giving up their babies for adoption have in common (this excludes surrogates) is that they are all people in crisis. Statistically speaking, I figured I was most likely writing to a teenager. I know they're having a lot of sex...so where's my baby?

My mother blames teen sex on cable television. "These kids see it on TV and think it's okay. I'm glad I'm not a mother in this day and age. You kids knew better." She was right. We did know better, though I don't know how we knew better. It's not like she or my stepfather ever gave us a poignant talk on the subject of sex. We just knew. Sex was for marriage. You saved yourself for the person you married. Not one guy who ever tried to put his hands in my blouse supported this plan. I supported the plan because the plan was really about worth. I was worth more as a virgin. That's what I was taught. If I wasn't a virgin, I had no market value and would never be treated well.

In high school I was in love with Mike Lund. We went to different schools so it wasn't an on-campus love affair. No stolen kisses behind locker doors or under bleachers. We used to park under a willow tree and make out. We used to go to his basement and make out some more. I loved kissing him, and I loved his stocky physique. When we made out he let the energy travel throughout his body. When we first met and we kissed, the kisses stayed on my lips; when we hugged, the hugs stayed on my skin and against my muscles. His body, however, had a life that mine was unaware of. My body had only known the language of sports. That was about to change.

Somewhere in the summer of my fifteenth year on earth, my sister and I were allowed to invite some friends up to our family cottage on a lake for the day. It was actually a trailer on a strip mine, but cottage sounds nicer. It was at a private club (it really was nice) called Shannon Shores and required a membership to get in. It was once a gigantic rock quarry. I imagined they took one too many rocks out and struck a spring. The hole filled up to form an impressive lake. The owner had the vision to see a future outside the rock and landfill business and turned the site into a resort. He sold plots with electricity hookups as well as trailers to the public, and before long there were dozens of trailers around his lake, each with its own pier. We called the owner Captain; it was my stepfather's idea. My parents bought into the club and for a couple of summers we went there to swim and water-ski. They mostly drank, which is probably why it only lasted a couple of summers.

We swam and drank beer and ate Jay's potato chips. I probably had two or three beers. Mike and I went into one of the bedrooms to make out. I'm not sure if it was the beer or our swimsuits, but my body was experiencing something it had never felt before. The kisses weren't staying on my lips. They were traveling throughout me. My hips began to sway up and down. I was shocked. What was happening to my body? It was the most amazing thing I'd ever felt. He wanted our clothes to come off. I didn't want to change a thing... so we didn't. I had my first orgasm at Shannon Shores (really, it was a nice resort), and my life would never be the same.

These were my thoughts as we drove back to Chicago later that day: "Why didn't anyone tell me about this? This is why people get up in the morning. How could

I not know my body could do this? Why didn't anyone tell me? How would you tell someone something like this, really? Now I know why people want to live and breathe." As the sun began its descent, I smiled at Mike in the rearview mirror and mouthed the words, "I love you."

At fifteen I had become a sexual being. Fortunately for me teen pleasure didn't become teen sex; therefore, it never became teen pregnancy. I believe I stopped that day with Mike and all the days that followed because I couldn't bring myself to give up my value for anyone or anything, not even Mike or love. Now, at almost forty, my value lies elsewhere. And though it's not flattering to admit, one thing hasn't changed. Sex is still a reason to get up in the morning. It's just not the only reason anymore. I have a mortgage now too. That's really all you need in life, two good reasons to get out of bed. Sex and a mortgage were enough for many years.

I hear teen sex is much different now. Apparently, a lot of teens don't think oral sex is sex. They think intercourse is sex and everything else is fooling around. And for some reason, today girls believe they're of more value if they are sexually active. Like it or not, girls, that's a lie. Because young girls believe the lie, there are a lot more teen pregnancies today than there were when I was a teen.

For years I supported educational programs that aspired to reduce teen pregnancy. Now, because I wanted a baby, I was for teen pregnancy; it was an unfortunate necessity. I would think, "Thank God those teenagers are having sex." And like my friend Ben said when he and his wife were waiting to adopt, "Those teenagers make the best-looking babies. When you're fifteen you're picking only the best-looking guys to go out with. Hell, your standards don't go down till you're in your late thirties."

It was the middle of June. I had signed on with Jane nine months earlier, I had revised my birth mother letter, and it was four months since my last nibble. I began to focus again on my work. I had five shows to do in Michigan. I opened my suitcase and hung my pantsuits in the hotel closet. I called my answering machine to pick up my messages. There was a message from The Agency. A birth mother had responded to my letter. The voice on the machine asked me to call them immediately.

Twenty

The Call

How life can change in one phone call...
or just be put on hold.

I THOUGHT my heartfelt letter and the photo essay that I'd put together would get good results. It was a short pictorial montage paralleling my life, I thought, with Mother Teresa's, without mentioning her of course. I took some creative liberties. For instance, to humanize myself I had to show her in a bad light. If it didn't work for the adoption, I figured I could recycle it at a later date and at least get some grant money.

Whenever I get an urgent message to call someone immediately, I immediately take some time for myself. Not a lot of time, just enough to settle down and put some starch in my ruffles. It's a Smith family tradition to remain unruffled. We also have a long history of killing the messenger, so news in general doesn't bode well with us. I usually don't need more than a day or two to quiet my nerves. Once I took three weeks, but I admit now that was a mistake. I didn't know he was

144

waiting at the gas station for me. That's a whole other story. This was about a baby. I didn't have a day or two. I took five minutes and called The Agency back.

My lawyer's assistant/wife, Linda, told me there was a birth mother in Wyoming who was placing her baby and might want to meet me tomorrow. I explained that I was in Ann Arbor and had shows to do that night and the next. "Are you saying I have to cancel my performances?" She said, "You might. We don't know yet. We're waiting for a call back from the birth mother's lawyer. We wanted to know whether you're interested first." I said, "Of course I'm interested. Tell me about the baby." She said, "Well, he's not a newborn." All I heard was, "It's a boy." My heart fluttered. Then I realized what else she had said. "He's not a newborn." That was a red flag.

I thought, okay, what grade is he in? The thing about kids is you want to get them before they're shaving. Older was not good. It could mean a "special needs" child. I had said on my application that I wasn't qualified to parent a "special needs" child. I knew this from experience. My Aunt Jean and Aunt Joan were twins. Jean and Joan. Jean had a daughter Suzie who was severely handicapped. Suzie was older than me but couldn't sit up on her own. She mostly lay on her back and looked around. Her mouth was always open and she thrashed involuntarily. Her body was pulled tight. She carried the tension of the entire family in her little body.

My sisters and I were told not to get too close to Suzie. My mother would warn, "If she gets ahold of you, she'll rip your hair out of your head." Aunt Joan would warn us as she bent over to change Suzie's diaper, "Stay back. She's strong. She doesn't know her own strength." Aunt Joan was much calmer than my mother was about Suzie, and Aunt Jean, Suzie's mother, was always the calmest. She seemed so peaceful.

I was afraid of Suzie. So were my sisters. My mother found the silver lining. She saw Suzie as an opportunity. She used Suzie to keep us out of harm's way. She told us we would end up like Suzie if we did certain things. If we walked too close to a swing she'd yell, "You're too close to that swing. You wanna get hit in the head? That's what happened to Suzie. She got hit in the head with a swing." It was Suzie who saved us from electric shocks, falls, choking, street traffic, and eating anything that wasn't in a wrapper. Every encounter has a gift.

"Special needs" can mean many things. It can be as simple as not having been handled enough or just needing to do some catching up. I hear a lot of that chatter around the Chinese baby girls whom Americans are racing to adopt.

My friend Lynn almost took custody of a beautiful little two-year-old girl who had been shaken. She still had a shunt in her head but was expected to fully recover. Lynn turned down that opportunity because she wasn't guaranteed that the state of California would allow her to adopt the baby. The state tries to keep the family unit together at a high cost to the children. It's a good thing to help the family work out their addictions and alcoholism. People need help recovering. I happen to believe, however, it should not be on the baby's time. I don't believe it's help if it's at the cost of even one single baby. Lynn couldn't take that baby because she knew it would be too much for her if she had to let the child go back into the family that had harmed her. And then there are babies who have been in the system long enough to have suffered abuses only they will ever know about. Their special needs are emotional and may include the need to steal your wallet.

I said, "How old is he?" She said, "He's eight months." To me that was a newborn. She said, "The birth mother is twenty-four. Her story is unusual. From what I can tell, it looks like the baby was in the care of a friend of hers for the first four months. He's been with her now for almost four. She started the adoption process about two months ago. There's no birth father involved. There was a boyfriend, but they broke up before the baby was born. She says she doesn't know where he is." I was trying to process the information as it was fed to me. There was a lot of information. I was whirling with excitement and trepidation. I said, "What do you think?" She said, "I think we won't know until you go there and meet them." I said, "Okay."

We hung up and I waited, as I was told to, for her to call me back. I called my manager and told her to stay near the phone. "I might have to leave for Wyoming before the show tonight." She had to be on hand to deliver the bad news to the club manager if I had to cancel my shows. That alone is reason for having a manager. They deliver all the bad news for you. There should be relationship managers.

Was this really going to happen? Was this it? It had been just over nine months, a very common gestation period for first-time mothers. I was due. Other than the lady from Social Services, it had been an easy pregnancy. I looked at my suitcase lying opened on the luggage stand. Good thing I'm still packed, I thought. I learned over the years to look around before unpacking. One time I carried the entire toilet seat to the front desk to tell them, "I've changed my mind." I had never been to Wyoming. I was sure it was "out West" though.

Linda from The Agency called back and told me I would not have to leave Michigan after all. It was going to take a few days for the birth mother's lawyer to generate the necessary paperwork to proceed. Linda told me I would most likely go to Wyoming the following weekend if all went well. In the meantime, The Agency thought it would be a good idea for the birth mother and me to talk on the phone. Linda would work on setting that up. "When is a good time for you?" she asked. I said, "I go home Sunday. How about Sunday afternoon?" That would give me two days to panic, access my higher self, panic some more, and so on. The Agency told me the birth mother grew up in the same part of Illinois as I did. I wondered whether she knew my family.

Twenty-One

Why Me?

*How my aversion to organized religion
and my Midwestern accent
made me mother material.*

I **THOUGHT** very little about my shows that weekend; they're just a vague memory. I was dreaming of that baby boy. He was all I could think about. What did he look like? What did the birth mother look like? Would I have to get a cell phone now? I supposed I would because I'd need to be reachable at all times if I got this baby. What if the birth mother didn't like me? Why wouldn't she? It was my job to make rooms full of strangers like me. She was just one more. One that mattered.

I returned home from Michigan on Sunday morning, unpacked, and started cleaning my house, which I had cleaned before I left for Michigan. I looked around the spare bedroom. Which wall should the crib go against? I didn't want to get too far into planning; for instance, I still didn't have a crib, in case it didn't happen. The

Agency had given me a number to call to talk to the birth mother. They didn't specify a time to call her. They said around midday. If the call went well, I would move on to the next step. I wondered what the next step was. When I asked The Agency, they said it would depend on her lawyer and how fast he got the paperwork done.

At noon, midday to those on a mission, I dialed the number The Agency had given me. It rang twice before a woman's voice answered, "Hello." I said, "This is Margaret Smith. Could I please speak to Carol?" "Hi. This is Carol." She sounded happy to hear from me. I told her I hoped it was a good time, and she immediately said, "You sound like everyone I grew up with." "Really," I said. That was good news to me because it was good news to her. I asked her where she grew up. When she told me where, I said, "I have relatives there. My uncle is a cop in that township."

What I didn't say was, "That's where my father got into an argument with a man and was shot three times. Once in the back and two more times when he turned around and faced the shooter." It was a working-class neighborhood outside Chicago. Back then it had no sidewalks. We lived in a neighboring township that had a few occasional sidewalks. We lived there very briefly.

Just long enough for my dad to get shot and die, not quite a year.

She told me her mother used to work in a travel agency there. "My parents don't live there anymore. They moved to Phoenix four years ago." She was really nice. I liked her, and she seemed to like me. I wasn't sure how to end the conversation but was certain it should be me to end it. I said, "I'm excited to meet you and the baby." I wanted to move forward. I would hear soon whether she felt the same way. I would call The Agency and tell them I was ready to fly to Denver the minute they said it was okay to go. Then I would wait for The Agency to let me know when Carol wanted me to drive to nearby Cheyenne meet her and her baby.

It was one of the most unusual meetings I had ever had on the phone and by far the most meaningful. The only phone encounter I had that ever came close to it, and it's really like comparing apples and deodorants, was with the strange man who called my parents' house in response to my sister Sue's "For Sale" ad in the *Penny Saver*. She was selling her very cool powder blue Ford convertible. This was back in the late sixties. I was the closest one to the phone when it rang. Six kids, what were the chances? He identified himself as being "interested in the car you placed in the *Penny Saver*." I said, "Oh, that's my sister's car. I'll get her." He said, "Maybe you could answer a couple of questions for me." I said, "Okay." It made me feel important. I was about to find out how little I really knew about my sister's car. It started out simple—the mileage, the year, the tires...were they worn?

Then it took a wrong turn. He moved to the interior of the car. I told him there were leather seats. That's when his voice changed. He asked, "Are they clean." I said, "Yes, she takes very good care of the car." He said, "I bet she does. Does she go on dates in it?" My thirteen-year-old face scrunched up. I said, "I don't know." "Well, does she fool around in there?" he asked. I thought he meant playing the radio and stuff. I said, "Yeah, there's a cool radio in it." He said, "Does she have sex with boys in there?" I became a hostage. I didn't want to be responsible for losing the sale, but I was afraid of him. I said, "I don't know what she does." He said, "Is there cum all over the seats?" I said, "You'll have to ask her." Then I yelled into the living room. "Suzie, telephone!" I don't know why I didn't just hang up. Maybe I thought if we could just get through this difficult period we could still make the sale.

Suzie came running. As I handed her the phone I said, "It's someone about your car." She put the phone to her ear. "Hello." After a quick pause she slammed the phone onto the receiver and glared at me. "What's wrong with you?" I said, "I didn't know what to do." I never asked her what he said. But I was impressed by how quickly she knew what he was up to.

Aside from the fact that they were both first times, the two telephone meetings had little in common. Both were memorable and both are in this book. If you can see anything else that may connect the two events, get a paper and pencil and send them to my publisher because I'm done paying for therapy. If you're the guy that called, I hope your cell mate is everything you ever wanted.

The adoption started to build momentum. I flew to Denver that weekend. It was the Fourth of July, Independence Day of all things. United Airlines had a round-trip special for two hundred dollars. I rented a car and checked into a hotel with a wagon wheel out front. It was clean and had a swimming pool inside. It was a big place, but as far as I could tell the only people staying there were me and an elderly man in a cowboy hat. The lady at the desk was eager to help me with directions and anything else I needed.

I got settled and called Carol. She was ready to meet me, but the baby was down for a nap. We would meet in one hour. It seemed like such a long time to wait. It turned out that an hour was barely enough time for me to get a child safety seat fastened into the rental car. There were no directions with it. It looked simple enough. I was missing one important tool, miniature hands. Although I'm a small woman, I do not possess the hands of a salamander. As I tried for the fifteenth time to feed the seat belt through the slits in the back of the safety seat, I had this thought: how do these women do it? It was the beginning of my respect and admiration for mothers.

It was a basement apartment in a two-flat building. We greeted each other with a smile and mutual nervousness. He was still sleeping. There were books everywhere. This was a well-read woman, college educated. She had the sniffles, allergies she explained. I wondered whether the baby would have allergies. It was dark down there. All the curtains were closed. She told me she kept it dark because she had an acute sensitivity to light. We talked easily. I asked her a lot of questions about her family, not because she was the birth mother but because I am always interested in a person's story. We may live many lives in a lifetime, but we have only one life story.

She showed me her family photo album and told corresponding stories as we moved from page to page. When we finished we went into her bedroom, also dark, and up against the wall in the corner was a little bed six inches off the ground with a net around it. It was the kind of bed you can bring out into the yard for cookouts. She bent over and lifted him out. He was awake. She turned on a light and laid him on her bed. He was absolutely beautiful. He had the biggest almond-shaped eyes I had ever seen, wisps of white blond hair, and a little mouth. She changed him into a dry diaper, and I followed her into the kitchen where she made him a bottle. She used soy infant formula. She explained that since she had allergies she thought it was best to give him soy just in case. She told me he might inherit her allergies. I told myself, not necessarily.

We moved back into the living room with the baby and the bottle. She asked whether I wanted to hold him. All I wanted to do was hold him. I'd flown all the way to Denver and driven to Cheyenne to hold him. She handed him over to me. I fed him the bottle and stared into his eyes. I wanted this baby. I knew the minute I saw him, this would be my baby. My heart was jumping rope and skipping down the sidewalk. She asked, "Would you like to take him out for a while?" When I heard myself say, "Yes," I got scared. I had never taken a baby out for a while or a minute.

She packed a bag for him with diapers and formula and wipes as I burped him. She put a change of clothes in there too. She said, "Would you like to change him?" "Sure," I said. I followed her into the bedroom and laid him on her bed. She handed me a diaper and sat on the edge of the bed. I removed the wet one and handed it to her. She watched as I figured out which end of the diaper went where. I felt as if I was taking a test and changing the diaper was an important part of my grade point average. I had to do it right or I wouldn't get the grade I needed to get this baby. She would doubt my abilities and change her mind before I got the diaper changed. It was so obvious that I was new at it. She had changed him with the ease of humming a song. I changed him like I was handcuffed.

He was ready to go and so was I. It was surreal. She trusted me to take him out into the world for a few hours. She was giving me the best gift in the entire world, a person, a little perfect boy whom I was so afraid of and whom I already loved. I felt weak and insignificant and chosen. I loaded him into the car seat just as awkwardly as I had put the diaper on him. I closed his door like I had never closed a car door before in my life, with great care. I walked around to the driver's side and opened the door. I think I said goodbye to Carol on my way. I think she told us to have fun. I was having a hard time listening.

I watched my every move as I prepared for take off. I didn't want to miss any safety procedures. On top of everything else, my surroundings felt awkward because it wasn't my car. It was a rental. I shifted into reverse and looked over my shoulder. He was still there in his seat. So far, so good. I had never driven with a baby in my car. Others had . . . many others. They let you know it too. They put notices in their back windows, Baby on Board. I used to see those and think, "what do you want me to do, lady, pull over and wait till you're home safe?" Now I wished I had one. I wanted to let other drivers know to slow down and watch out for my car. I was carrying precious cargo. I looked out the rear window and backed out of the driveway. She watched as we drove away. I think we had agreed that I'd be back with him at 6:00 p.m.

I took him to a park and we fed the ducks. He loved watching the ducks eat bread. I found a tree to sit under and began playing with him in the grass. It was a beautiful lawn, the kind you can't find in southern California. He hated it. He didn't want the grass to touch him. I went to plan B. I spread out a blanket I had borrowed from the hotel and put him on that. It was much better. Then I gave him a Pepperidge Farm Milano cookie. I was sure that was something you did with babies. Who doesn't give a baby cookies? He held onto it with both hands. The chocolate mortar that holds the two wafers together soon covered his face. When the remaining part of the cookie was what I guessed to be choking hazard size, I took it from him, wiped his face, which he didn't like, and fed him a bottle.

I had never filled time with a baby. I was happy to just sit in the park and stare at him for the hours we had. But I thought I should give him experiences. Hopefully new ones, which would be ours. I took him swimming at the hotel. I was nervous during the whole twenty minutes.

What if he pooped in the pool? I had a diaper on him, but how would I know? It was hard to tell how he felt about being in water. He wasn't laughing. He didn't cry. He didn't splash or seem curious either. He was kind of lethargic, but compared to what?

He was eight months old and made no sounds. No oohs or ahhs. I wasn't sure if he should be making noises. Well, maybe I was getting just what I wanted. I had prayed for compatibility; maybe that's just what I'd get. I'm not a chatty person and neither was he. I enjoy listening and so did he. I like quiet time as much as he did.

When I brought him back, Carol asked whether I'd like to see how she gave him a bath. I was ecstatic to get the invitation. It meant I was still in the running. I watched as she explained how the water should be tepid, what soap to use, how to sponge the soap off, how to wash his hair, of which he had little, and how to towel him dry. It was sweet.

She mentioned they were running low on formula and baby food. I gave her some of both. She mentioned they were running low on funds. I wrote her a check for her rent and left. I lay awake that night and worried about him. Would he run out of food before I saw him again? Would she pick me? I had already picked him. I'd have to wait to hear from my lawyer.

My lawyer and her lawyer spent the next week going back and forth about money and other legalities. I was a wreck. Would he blow this? Would she back out? Was the baby eating? Finally my lawyer called with good news. "Congratulations. She wants to move forward with the adoption. You can call and talk to her now." I had wanted to call her. I wanted to check on the baby. I hadn't slept well since meeting him. I was worried about him. Was this what it was going to be like? I would turn into a worrier. I would become my mother. I called Carol as soon as I hung up the phone.

The first thing she told me was that he had been sick since I brought him back. He had contracted a bad rash and a cold. I remembered the grass. He knew more than I did, I thought. Four hours with him and I had made him sick. We talked a while. I was happy and she seemed happy. She had found a place for her baby. She felt good about it. It seemed okay to ask, so I did. "Why did you pick my letter?" She said, "I liked what you said about God. I didn't want some Bible thumper raising him." I couldn't remember exactly what I had said about God. I remembered I had said I didn't belong to any organized religion but had forgotten the rest. She said, "And when we talked on the phone, you sounded like where I came from."

When we hung up I went into my files and pulled out my birth mother letter. I had written, "I lead a God-conscious life."

Twenty-Two

Bringing Home My Son

How I got ready for his arrival
right after I brought him home.

I **THOUGHT** traveling with a baby would be like having an extra piece of luggage. And it is. You just can't set it down anywhere. I had to pee so bad I couldn't wait another exit or another minute. I pulled off the highway somewhere between Cheyenne and the Colorado border. I was on the lam, and my back hurt from the rental car I was driving. My lawyer had told me that I wasn't supposed to leave the state of Wyoming for forty-eight hours. I never really understood why. Something about the paperwork wasn't finished for an interstate adoption. It was totally legal that I had him, I just wasn't supposed to cross state lines with him yet. I hadn't reached the state line, but I felt like Richard Kimbal because I was headed there.

I got out of my economy-sized rental car and straight-
ened myself up. It was then that I realized I couldn't just
run through the truck stop and into the bathroom like
I used to. I looked at him through the back door window. He was sleeping. I opened his door, unclipped the
harness that held him in his seat (it looked more uncomfortable than mine), and picked him up. He slept on my
shoulder as I raced toward the restroom. I got in the stall
and closed the door. That's when the reality of being in
the world with a baby hit me. How can I get my pants
down with a baby in my arms? There was nowhere to put
him, just a hook on the back of the door. That wasn't
an option. He didn't even own a pair of suspenders. I
never had noticed how small and ill-equipped a public
restroom stall was before.

I started to pee. The way my bladder works is, if it
thinks it's going to get emptied, a thirty-second internal timer starts and it takes an intervention by the
urethra to stop it. Only a little came out. Oh, the body
is a wonderful thing if you take care of it. A zipper
would have been easy. Naturally, I was wearing button-
down jeans. The baby was now awake. It was probably
the swearing that woke him. I held onto him tight with

one arm and unbuttoned my pants with my free hand. I then managed to get them down far enough to sit. He sat on my lap and studied his new surroundings. I wanted to tell him, "This isn't where we'll be living" but didn't because I was still laboring under the delusion that you don't talk to people who can't understand you. That, by the way, was the hardest adjustment for me to make when I became a mother. A no-hands trip to the restroom in button-down pants was easy compared to what lay ahead of me, the job of narrating the world for someone.

It was a good thing I had such a hard time getting my pants down because it was the only thing that could have prepared me for the more difficult job of getting them back up. It's not that hard to button a blouse with one hand, but jeans require holding the two halves together. The material is thicker and less compliant. I waited a while for someone to come into the restroom, anyone, so I could ask them to button my pants for me. That's how desperate I was. I'm sure they would have declined when I refused to let them hold the baby instead of struggling with my barn door. Letting someone hold him so soon after I got him was not an option.

I got mad and swiveled my right hip out, slung him over it, wrapped my arm around him (in yoga it's called Restroom with Baby pose), and buttoned my pants with both hands.

I was back on the road in no time. Heading where, though? I had told the birth mother not two hours ago that she could reach me at the hotel if she needed to. I didn't know it was a lie until I heard it come out of me. I went directly to my hotel room, packed my bags and my baby, and up and left without a discernible thought in my head. My body didn't want to stop moving. Now it was getting dark out, and I was on my way to catch a plane that wouldn't leave till the next day with a baby I couldn't go pee with. I had performed in Denver many times. Surely I knew someone who could provide a safe haven for my baby and myself for one night. I could have gone to a hotel near the airport, but I didn't want to be alone. I needed to be with someone.

I called a friend of a friend who ran a chain of health food stores in Colorado, Liz. I had met her a couple of times and really liked her. She sold me a juicer a couple of years back. She was sleeping with a friend of mine so she sold it to me for cost. She was a generous soul and a very dedicated single mother, and I needed one of those not for the baby, for me. I needed a mother. I knew she would be open to my new baby and me so I called her. She didn't hesitate to offer us her home for the night. I believed she felt honored. She gave me directions to her house. It felt good to have a destination. I drove high up into the mountains to Evergreen, Colorado.

I thought there would be better accommodations at her ranch. I hear "ranch," I picture the Ponderosa, Hoss, Little Joe. There wasn't even a table set for dinner, let alone Hop Sing. She had a spare room, but there was nothing in it, not even a bed, just a couple of boxes and a blast of cold air that hit me in the face when she opened the door. It's cold in the evening up in the mountains in July. We talked for a while and passed the baby back and forth. Her son stayed in his room on the computer. I had met him once before when he was around nine. Now he was a teenager. Every once in a while he walked into the kitchen talking to a girl on the phone and grabbed something to eat. I knew it was a girl because he was thrilled silly to be explaining himself. "No, that's not what I meant. Who told you that? He's so low he could jump off a dime." I thought, this is probably a sneak preview of what's to come. Girls and food and a fluttering heart.

It was starting to get late. Liz brought out an inflatable mattress and began blowing it up. I wasn't sure if it was for her or her son or me and the baby. I was hoping to provide a bed for the baby. It was our first night together. In between breaths she explained that she had to get up early the next morning, that her staff was in the middle of doing a yearly inventory at her main store. "There are boxes everywhere." She puffed into the nozzle between thoughts. "Customers can't even walk down the aisles." I felt for her. It's hard enough to remember to take vitamins let alone having to count how many you have left. She did have beautiful skin. I wondered if it was the clean mountain air or the supplements she took. It certainly wasn't from sleeping on an air mattress because she gave that to me and my baby to sleep on.

It was about two in the morning. Half the air was out of the mattress. The good thing about slow leaks is they let you down easy. The sharp parts of my body like my hips and my elbows could feel the hardwood floors every time I rolled over. I knew it was two in the morning was because the baby started crying and I got up to make him a bottle. He didn't want it so I opened a jar of baby food. He wouldn't eat it. He cried more. I got the Pooh Bear his birth mother had sent with him. I had asked her for two things, his bear and his blanket, and asked her not to wash them. I wanted a familiar smell for him as a transitional tool.

He wanted none of it. I changed his diaper. He kept crying. I patted his back, and when that didn't work I began singing to him and then talking to him. I told him not to be scared, that I would never let anything hurt him. I told him where we were and that this wasn't our home. We would go to our home in the morning and he would love it, I told him. "It has a big yard with two dogs, Molly and Jack, and we can go to the park and hike if you want," I said as I held him. He could not be comforted. I laid him across my knees and rubbed his back in a circular motion because I heard my mother's voice, "It's probably gas."

Nothing I did worked that first night together. I couldn't take away his loss. I could understand it. I lost my father before I had the grown-up words to describe loss. Loss without words is a bottomless pit of fear. I don't remember why he stopped crying. It had started to get light out, that much I remember. I think he just got tired. It was one of the most powerless moments of my adult life. It was also a guided moment because I didn't know how to be his mother. I had chosen him as my son, but he had not chosen me as his mother yet. Part of my plan was to wait for him to pick me. What I would do to help him decide I hadn't really thought about. That night I had to be a sieve and let his feelings go through me so I could contain him. I told myself that he had a God of his own, just like I do, who takes care of him and knows a lot more about him than me.

We got up early and headed for the airport. The car rental place gave us a ride from their lot to our terminal. When I asked for a child safety seat for the baby, the driver looked bewildered. "You can't put a kid's seat in there. It's a minibus. There's no seat belts." Then he got in, pulled the door closed, and fastened his seat belt. I couldn't believe the thoughtlessness of the vehicle's designers. I was appalled. No child safety seats and no way to secure one. I would never rent from them again.

I held the baby as the driver got our bags from the luggage rack on board. I gave him a tip. It wasn't his fault. He just worked there. If you've never been to the Denver International Airport, it's huge. You have to take trains to get from one terminal to another. Once inside a terminal, you still have a walk ahead of you. I like walking; it's carrying luggage that bogs me down. I had one bag on wheels and one to carry. I hooked one onto the other and looked for a cart. I managed to get six quarters out of my purse and into the quarter slots. I yanked a cart from the machine and put my bags on it. When I went to set the baby in the seat, there was nowhere for his legs to go through. It would only accommodate a purse or maybe a small briefcase. I thought that I must have imagined seeing parents push their kids around in those things at airports. I could feel anger rising up inside me. I was still tired from the night before. Would it have been a lot more work and money to put some holes in this purse holder for a little pair of baby's legs to fit through? One more step in the manufacturing process was too much to ask? I finished my internal rant with "that's what's wrong with this country."

Both of us slept on the flight home. I woke up before him and found that he had slid, wrapped in his blanket, from my lap, down my two legs, and into the crook of my two ankles. It made me laugh. He faced me with his back on the tops of my feet. He was beautiful. I reached

down and slid him onto my lap. I walked him around
the plane and showed him things. He was happy to do
that. He seemed to be taking it all in. I have a curious
baby, I thought. I gave him a bottle as we were landing.
My mother had told me to do that so his ears wouldn't
hurt from the change in pressure. "Make sure he's hungry when you take off and land or he'll scream." She
knew a few things.

Lisa was waiting for me when I got off the plane. She
was a wreck. "I've been worried sick. Are you sure you
know what you've gotten yourself into? Let me see him.
Ahh." As soon as I saw a luggage cart, I looked to see
whether it had leg holes for babies. It did. I was re-
lieved to learn that I lived near a good airport. That was
a new thought. I have so many of the same thoughts all
the time that I notice when there's a new one. A new
thought is noticeable like a new kid on the block is noticeable. Would I be having a lot of them? That thought
scared me. A lot of new thoughts meant a lot of not
knowing what to do. Would the world be forever different now that I was in this new group of people? I was a
mother—more specifically, a single mother.

My mind was home before me. I had enough to do to
get through a day or two with him. I had bought a crib

before I went to get him, also a buggy, a car seat, and some diapers. My baby was here. I guessed it was time to have a baby shower. What would I call it? It wasn't really a shower. In that sense, it had already rained. I'd call it a welcoming party. But first, I just needed to get him home.

Twenty-Three

AKA

How naming my son made me his mother.

I THOUGHT he had experienced enough loss without me changing his name. My higher self told me to let him keep his original name, to honor his brief history in this world. It was a beautiful name. I would grow to love it because I loved him and it was the right thing to do. That lasted about a week. I didn't know if I was getting off my high horse or on it. I did know that I couldn't live with him forever without saying his name.

I would say his name if someone asked what his name was. When I pushed him around the neighborhood in his buggy, he would get a lot of comments about how beautiful he was. "He's so beautiful. What's his name?" I'd say his name and wonder what it meant. Or if we went to the park. The sandbox is a hot spot of adoring mothers. I don't know how they do it, those mothers. They adore their babies and then they take a time out from all that adoration to adore my baby. I didn't seem to share their abundance of adoration.

I seemed to adore only my baby. I thought he was the most beautiful and the smartest and the brightest light in the sandbox. I would say something in return to complete the exchange, but it was never, "She's so beautiful." It was usually something more along the lines of, "What's his name? How old is he? Boy, he looks so alert. He must be smart."

My last experience in a kids' park was in Nashville when I needed pictures of me with children to send along with my birth mother letter. I was an uncomfortable outsider then. Now I was an uncomfortable insider. I was learning sandbox etiquette. It didn't take me long to figure out that when a mother asked me how old my baby was she was also asking how long I'd had to get my body back in shape. I never got tired of hearing, "He's only nine months? You look great." I'd say, "Thank you." Why go into a lot of detail with a stranger about his birth? My lower self was fine accepting a compliment at the expense of their self-esteem. Hell, maybe I was doing them a favor. Maybe they would pick up the pace a little on their morning walk.

I also noticed they would gauge how well their kid was doing developmentally compared to mine. If my son and I had had a traditional beginning, I might have fallen into that awful experiment. I didn't because I knew it would be like comparing apples and couches. I knew he was incomparable because he had such a different beginning from a lot of other kids in the sandbox. Interrupted attachment is what I call it. I was totally absorbed in getting to know him. That I had no one to compare him to only helped clear my vision.

There is nothing that'll get in the way of knowing someone more than not knowing their name. I knew how to say his name and spell it, but that was it. I couldn't find a place inside me to put it. My higher and lower selves were exhausted. Deadlocked. I had to resolve it soon. It wasn't that I disliked his name. I liked it. It just held no meaning for me. I knew another guy who had the same name. I liked him. He was smart, handsome, and a good writer. It was a cool name. But it was a name that on some level I felt was being forced on me. My baby had been given a fine name, and his middle name was one I had considered as a first name when I fantasized about being a mother. But that was different. That was before I became a mother. That was before I felt like a mother and saw the world as a mother and had scary mother thoughts like "How will I ever stop swearing?"

Every time I thought his name, I felt his birth mother in the room with us. He was almost nine months old. I asked Susan if he knew what his name was at this age. She said he knew it as a sound and asked, "What are you thinking of naming him?" I said, "George, after my father." She said, "Well, his birth name is a 'J' sound too so it won't be a huge change for him if you do it soon."

My baby and I had something in common. We both had early childhood losses. I think that's why I struggled with the decision so much. I knew what it felt like to have things taken away. But worse than that, I knew what it was like to have someone you loved be replaced. When my father died, my mother remarried two months later. My father, George, was replaced by Jim. I was old enough to know my father as more than a "J" sound. They had the same last name too because they were brothers. When I stopped talking for a year, my mother would sometimes respond for me. "This one's name is Margaret, but we call her Peggy. She's my quiet one." I never got comfortable saying "That's my dad" or calling my stepfather "Daddy."

At first my sisters and I called him what we knew him as, Uncle Jim. That was not well received. We lived in the South then where no one knew us. Mommy married

to Uncle Jim was not a good first impression. My sister
Kathy remembers that we were punished if we slipped
and called him "Uncle Jim." She said he would hit us.
My mother wanted us to get it right too. She didn't want
people to know "our business."

There were no pictures of my father on display in our
home after his death. They were kept in my mother's
cedar chest, a hope chest gone wrong. They wouldn't
surface for another thirty years, after my stepfather,
Jim, died. Only then would my sisters and I get a framed
picture of our father. It was a Christmas gift. It had
to be restored because a house fire had damaged the
photo, destroying one of his hands in the picture. My
mother had a new hand added digitally. It must have
been one of those discount digital places because one
hand looks relaxed and the other one looks like a small
oven mitt.

I wish I could tell you that I opened the gift and
said, "There really is a Santa Claus," but that wasn't
my response. I was able to feel happy for my mother,
who would now have the luxury of grieving my father's
death. It was as though a thirty-year interruption had
ended. The biggest pregnant pause of my life, and perhaps hers too, was over. My response, however, was to

remember. To remember is to let in all similar information and feelings. My response was to remember a Christmas past. It was the night that Santa died.

It was Christmas Eve, 1959. My father had died two years before. Some of my parents' close friends and all of our relatives had braved the cold and snow to gather at our house for a holiday celebration. There were about twenty adults and fifteen kids. My parents' bed was covered with a mound of winter coats that spilled onto the floor. My mother served food and drinks with a busy smile between rolling out dough and stirring the custard for her homemade lemon meringue pies. Piles of homemade Christmas cookies and trays of finger foods prepared by all the aunts were set out. Christmas decorations were set up throughout the house. Next to the tree on a small table was the only sign of my mother's side of the family, a bent-up plastic Hanukah bush.

My sisters and cousins and I ran through the house playing games of chase and hide-and-seek, stopping only to snitch on one another about an injustice or to ask about Santa.

Every once in a while I would run up to my mom and ask, "When's Santa getting here?" Well, multiply that by fifteen kids and you can see it was asked quite often that night. As my aunts and uncles became more and more intoxicated, I'm sure we asked more and more, "When's Santa coming? When is Santa coming here? Is Santa coming soon?" Somewhere in our little intelligent brains, we must have sensed that the chances of Santa showing up for a bunch of drunks was slim.

Several of my uncles were Chicago policemen so I was accustomed to seeing men wearing guns. That's how I sometimes figure out how old I was when I remember incidents from my childhood. How tall was I compared to the guns? This particular Christmas I almost came up to their holsters; I was five years old. My Uncle Rich, who was my godfather, not an actual uncle, wasn't a cop; he was a truck driver who loved to hunt. So he didn't carry a revolver. He usually kept his hunting rifles at home in his bedroom closet. He was the craziest of all the uncles. I overheard him when he told his daughter, my cousin Cookie, "Don't ask me about Santa again. If you kids ask about Santa Claus one more time, I'm gonna kill him and then there won't be any presents. Is that what you want?" She of course said, "No." Word spread quickly throughout the kid population at the Christmas party. We all knew and agreed not to ask again, "When is Santa gonna get here?"

When the stakes were that high we wouldn't forget. I patrolled the perimeters of the party and kept my eyes and ears peeled. It got later and later and we got tired like kids do, and when kids get tired they get sloppy. I don't remember who, but one of us asked a grown-up, "Is Santa almost here?" And from across the room we heard Uncle Rich say, "That's it, I'm gonna kill the fat son of a bitch. Where's my gun?" He walked out of the house, slamming the front door behind him. One of the older kids went to the window to watch. After a few seconds he turned and reported, "He's opening his trunk." A mother's voice yelled, "Get out of that window."

Some of the kids started to whimper and were covered with a blanket of mother voices reassuring them it was all a joke. "Uncle Rich is just kidding." Two seconds later we heard two shots fired. The entire party went silent, and we heard another two shots. A moment later Uncle Rich walked through the front door with his shotgun slung over his shoulder. The other drunk uncles asked, "Did you get him?" Uncle Rich said, "I got the fat bastard. He's dead. Santa's dead." All the kids cried, "Santa's dead, Mommy, Uncle Richie killed Santa." And Uncle Rich added, "And I got a couple of his reindeer too."

It took me years to have a good Christmas again. As an adult I've had well over twenty of them now, and only a couple were bad ones. If that's the score when all is said and done, I'll be able to say, "Not bad." In the meantime I'll do my very best to make sure my son doesn't find out the truth about Santa from a bunch of gun-happy drunks.

As unsure as I was about what was proper, I decided to name my son George after my father because it felt good. Sometimes my higher self and my lower self are of no use to me and I go forward on blind faith. The universe will support me or not or give me a free pass. It was only after I named my son that I realized naming him was my first decision as a mother. In a sense it is the single action that defined me as his mother. It felt good to say, "My son, George." Later, when he can understand, I'll be able to tell him he was named after my father, after his grandfather, instead of telling him, "That's the name you had when we met."

My mother was upset at first when I told her I named him George. She said, "I don't know why you want to do that when your father died so tragically." I said, "That doesn't mean some good can't come out of it. Maybe because of the way his grandfather died, he'll be inspired to be a great doctor and save lives." My mother was right about one thing. I wasn't just giving my son a name. I was giving him a story. The stories we give to our kids are the stories that define them until they can tell their own story. It defines how they feel about themselves and how they see themselves in the world with all the other stories they cross paths with. I believe his name has a strong story, a story that offers a family, a lineage, and a sense of belonging. From that he can create his own story.

THE END

Acknowledgments

My gratitude goes to Sandra Newton, without whom I would not have been inspired to write this book.

It also goes to my sons, George and Cooper, for letting me go off so many mornings to write while they went to the park without me, and to Melissa Minton for never complaining and taking them to the park even when she didn't feel like it, even when she hated me.

I thank my three sisters, Kathy, Suzie, and Debby, who I share so many memories with. We each have different memories, I'm sure, but all of our memories have one thing in common, the human condition.

Lisa Noonan, my friend and manager, was instrumental in this labor of love, for offering her home and office and printer and advice and food (not the best because she doesn't eat fat or sugar), and let's not forget the whopping three-thousand-dollar advance she got me. Not bad for three years of my life. You want to play hardball? Call her. Thank God this book had nothing to do with money.

Speaking of money and God, I owe a world of thanks to Roy M. Carlisle, my editor, for mentoring me through the process of putting this book in your hands. He dragged me into and out of three publishing companies while he went through his midlife crisis.

Thanks to Dale de la Torre, my tenacious attorney, that three-thousand-dollar check cleared without incident.

I owe my friend Barbara Miletich a huge favor for her time and expertise. She convinced me to wear the see-through blue blouse for the cover of this book. Where would either of us be without Photoshop?

Finally, a heartfelt, humble bow to all the single moms out there. I wrote this book for every one of you who ever felt like you were only half of something. My hope is that you not spend another day living that apologetic existence, and experience the glory of being your children's whole world.

About the Author

MARGARET SMITH began her comedy career studying at the famed Second City Theater in Chicago. "After getting enough parking tickets to paper a small bathroom," she left Chicago and moved to New York, where she began performing at local comedy clubs. It was only a few years on the New York club scene before she was spotted by one of David Letterman's talent scouts and invited to make her first appearance on national television.

Her acerbic wit and delivery have made her popular with the press, as well as an invited guest on numerous late-night shows and specials. The American Comedy Awards presented her with the Funniest Female Stand-Up Comic Award in 1996. She has performed throughout the United States as well as in Montreal, Amsterdam, Australia, and Queen's Theatre, London. She is a regular on the Letterman, Leno, and Conan O'Brien shows. Her first live CD, *As It Should Be,* was released in 2000. Ms. Smith has been a staff writer on Greg Kinear's NBC talk show, *The Stephanie Miller Show*, and head writer for *The Roseanne Show*. She has done a season as a regular on the Fox network's *That 80's Show* and is now a staff writer for *The Ellen Show*.

A Word from the Editor

It became our "place" to meet. An odd restaurant called
the French Market Café, which was a café within a faux
French quarter building with little boutiques around
three sides of the indoor "square." Actually it is hard to
describe accurately, and even an odder place to visit,
situated as it is right on Santa Monica Blvd. in West
Hollywood in the midst of normal stores and shops. I
have even seen celebrities eating there at the outdoor
sidewalk tables for all to ogle. Usually they are character actors or older stars who don't care if fans recognize
them because they are just enjoying themselves and if
a fan interrupts their meal for an autograph or a hello,
it is all taken in gracious stride. If you live in the West
Hollywood area, as my daughter Vanessa did for a few
years, this odd café becomes a kind of landmark. My favorite meal there with her was breakfast but that is just
because breakfast is my favorite meal at all times, and
they serve a wonderful one. In the world of restaurant

chic it is odd to have a hotspot be a café with a huge menu that will accommodate any taste, with everything from a vintage kitsch shop to a gift shop with erotic cards situated around the perimeter with the café tables in the center. So there is something for everyone, but certainly this is not a hip place in the superficial sense of that word and it is never so busy that you can't get seated for whatever meal at whatever time you happen by, although it is always bustling. And the "wait" staff is always friendly.

Lisa Noonan, Margaret's agent, the ever present monitor of all things important to monitor, and one of the nicer people you could meet, would find a time for us to gather and the book talk would begin. Lisa is one of those agents whose warm and reasonable personality cuts across the grain of dazed and driven "agent" people in this land of quirky and relentlessly trying to be hip TV / film / music / celebrityville. She just made sure Margaret and I could do our editor/author business easily and then followed up with whatever needed to be done.

We certainly had met at other places over the years, but the French Market Café was the most quirky and fun place and it made it easy to schedule our periodic sessions on what needed to be done next on the manuscript and by whatever deadline. Somehow Margaret, a normal but brilliant comedy writer, had carved out a real life for herself in this world. A life where she raised her boys, lived her life, wrote for TV, did her amazing stand-up routines, and wrote a book. I am honestly in awe of how she did all of that. And I am in awe of how Lisa managed everything that went along with all of what Margaret did.

But lost in the mist of time is how we all got together. It has been a long road, and I had dragged Lisa and Margaret through two other publishing houses before we finally arrived here at Crossroad in New York, and the book finally became a real object, in your hands. I had my times of wondering if that could ever happen. But after watching Margaret actually do her stand-up act live at a club in San Francisco a few years ago, I knew I was going to work very hard to make this book happen even if the odds were against us. Humor that is neither scatological nor cruel is more rare in stand-up than you might imagine. At least it is from my perspective, after visiting many comedy clubs in Los Angeles, San Francisco, Chicago, and New York. Margaret's humor made me laugh, of course, and laugh hard, but it also was insightful about human relationships in a way that was endearing and authentic. My editorial instinct was that her humor and her authenticity would work in a book, and they do.

If you listen to Margaret's CD, *As It Should Be*, and meet her in person, well maybe on the TV or in a sitcom (she was in *That 80s Show*), you are drawn to her because she is so real and so much herself. Put simply, I just like her and I like working with her, and I like what she has to say. I want men and women to read her book because it is fun and it is thoughtful. And I want everyone to experience humor that makes life a bit more bearable and a bit more hopeful. If Margaret and Lisa and I and the Crossroad team have accomplished that with this book then we have fulfilled our mission one more time admirably, as writer, agent, editor, and publishing staff.

Roy M. Carlisle
Senior Editor

Of Related Interest

T. Wyatt Watkins
WHAT OUR KIDS TEACH US ABOUT PRAYER

We're all accustomed to hearing about prayer from mystics, preachers, and spiritual masters, but what if we could learn from listening to our children? In *What Our Kids Teach Us About Prayer*, Reverend Watkins looks at the struggles we all endure as we try to pray and shows how children lead us out of those struggles with their candor, humor, and willingness to say absolutely whatever is on their minds!

0-8245-2319-9, $17.95, paperback

Please support your local bookstore,
or call 1-800-707-0670 for Customer Service.

For a free catalog, write us at

THE CROSSROAD PUBLISHING COMPANY
16 Penn Plaza — 481 Eighth Avenue, Suite 1550
New York, NY 10001

Visit our website at
www.crossroadpublishing.com
All prices subject to change.

crossroad